COLORWORK KNITTING

FROM HEAD TO TOE

20 STRANDED KNITTING PATTERNS FOR COLORFUL ACCESSORIES

CARMEN JORISSEN

DAVID & CHARLES
— PUBLISHING —

www.davidandcharles.com

Foreword

I'm overjoyed that you're holding my first ever knitting book, Colorwork Knitting From Head To Toe. In this book I hope to inspire you with my favourite knitting technique: colourwork knitting. Colour is absolutely fundamental for my knitted pieces and it's no secret that I'm known for my many-coloured knits. I've been addicted to knitting ever since first trying it in 2011, and my enthusiasm has only grown since then, especially after learning how to knit with more than one colour at a time.

Stranded colourwork uses two colours in the same row which allows you to create beautiful motifs. How a pattern can change by using different colours will never cease to amaze me, which is why I want to encourage you to choose your own colour palettes. Knit outside the box! You can find helpful tips for putting together colour combinations in Chapter 2: Choosing Colours.

In this book you will find 20 knitting patterns which all use the stranded colourwork technique. Five hats, five cowls, five pairs of mittens and five pairs of socks. Will you make a cowl with matching hat and mittens, or will you mix and match?

The colourwork motif designs in this book are all named after cities and towns in the Netherlands that I've called my home at some point in my life: Wessem, Haelen, Leiden, Heerlen and Urmond. During the designing process I've kept beginner knitters as well as advanced knitters in mind. Some motifs are more suitable for beginners while others will pose more of a challenge.

While reading this book you'll find some personal touches hidden here and there. Having my own knitting book is quite a milestone in and of itself, and being able to weave in some nostalgic elements made it all the more special to me.

Creativity runs in my family, and being surrounded by so many creative spirits my whole life has really made an impact on me. They have always been so supportive of me exploring a creative career, even though I studied something completely different. To honour them, I've placed some family Easter eggs throughout the book. An apple here and there to commemorate my grandpa who had an orchard, and some of my grandma's haberdashery notions. The idyllic Leudal forest where I've spent countless summer days with my mum, as she did with hers.

Knitting is a hobby for all generations, and the things we make are often passed down to others. I hope this book will encourage you to explore your creativity for years to come.

Carmen

Contents

Happy Knitting!

MAAS
WOL
Meter
WOL

Chapter 1

MATERIALS

Scheepjes
Scheepjes

YARN

Stranded colourwork can be compared to painting with yarn in many glorious colours. But before we discuss colour, let's delve into which yarns to use for the patterns in this book.

Some yarns work very well for stranded colourwork, while others are more tricky to knit with. Knitting stranded colourwork is easiest when using yarns that consist of mostly wool fibres. When looking at wool through a microscope, you see dozens of tiny little hooks that interlock when the wool is knitted into fabric. You might think 'that's all very well, but what does that mean for knitting colourwork?' When you alternate between using one colour and the other, the colour you are not using forms strands at the back of your work. The little hooks make sure that the yarn stays put more easily, which is not only helpful while wearing your knitted item, but also evens out your stitch tension.

Alternatively you can use acrylic yarns for stranded colourwork. The only yarns I would advise against are yarns of mostly plant based fibres, such as cotton and bamboo. Plant based yarns are much smoother, which makes it much more difficult to achieve an even tension.

Make it easy for yourself and choose a yarn with a high wool content. For this book I've used my all time favourite yarn Scheepjes Metropolis, which is 75% fine merino wool and 25% nylon, and has 200 metres per 50 grams. The added nylon makes the yarn stronger so your items will last longer. Scheepjes Metropolis is really soft and I've been using it for years. And - perhaps even most importantly - it comes in 80 different colours, which makes it an absolute treat to create colour palettes with. Find tips and tricks in Chapter 2: Choosing Colours.

KNITTING NEEDLES

There is wide range of different knitting needles, which can be quite overwhelming for newer knitters. Which type of knitting needle you end up using largely depends on personal preference. Do you knit with fixed or interchangeable circular needle, with a long or shorter cable, metal or bamboo needletips? Or do you prefer using double-pointed needles? With such a variety of knitting needles, here is what you need to know.

Circular needles

All of the patterns in this book can be knitted on a circular needle 80cm (32in) long, which is why they are my favourite needles to use! The magic loop method makes it possible to knit with a long needle, even if the circumference of what you're knitting is small, such as with a sock.

Alternatively, you can knit your project on a circular needle that is just right for your project. The hat and cowl patterns can be knitted on a circular needle 40cm (16in) long, without having to use the magic loop technique. Please do note that for the hat you will need to change to a longer cable or double-pointed needles in order to decrease for the crown, as it simply won't work on a 40cm (16in) cable. You could knit the socks on a very short circular needle of 20-25cm (8-10in) length, but you will need a longer circular needle or double-pointed needles for the toe.

Learning how to knit magic loop allows you to knit the entire project on the same needle throughout, which is so helpful. I cannot recommend it enough! This way you can invest in high quality needles to make knitting even more enjoyable, since you'll only ever need one per needle size. Find the magic loop instructions In Abbreviations and Techniques: Magic Loop Knitting.

Double-pointed needles

If you haven't worked with circular needles before or if you're simply not a fan, you might prefer using double-pointed needles. Double-pointed needles are used in sets of four or five and have a point on each end. The advantage of using them is that you can often knit your entire project with the same set, whereas with circular needles that may involve either magic loop knitting or switching between different lengths of needle. No matter if you have 100 stitches for knitting the cowl or just 10 for casting on a sock, it's no problem for double-pointed needles.

Metal, wooden or bamboo

Knitting needles come in various different materials, with the most common being metal, wood or bamboo. My personal preference is using metal needles since the stitches slide across the needles easily, which allows me to knit faster. The downside of metal needles is that it's easy to drop a stitch if you're not careful. The opposite is true for wooden and bamboo needles; the stitches glide less freely along these types of needle and are less likely to drop off. Metal needles are often sharper than bamboo or wooden ones, which allows you to do complex stitches like decreases more easily but also increases the chances of splitting your yarn.

Most knitters have a strong preference for using one type of needle over the other. If you have only tried one type of knitting needle so far I do recommend giving other types a try. One more piece of advice: don't switch to a different needle material within a project, since that can significantly affect your tension.

STITCH MARKERS

Stitch markers are great little tools, it's a good idea to have a couple of them handy while knitting. They are often circular so you can pop them on your knitting needles and use them to indicate the start of a round or the beginning of the pattern repeat. You don't need to go out and buy markers, you can also tie a piece of yarn in a circle and use those instead.

TAPESTRY NEEDLES

To finish off your project you will need a tapestry needle, and it's even better if you have a sharp one as well as a blunt one. Sharp tapestry needles are great for weaving in ends because you can split the fabric you're weaving into, which keeps your yarn ends more secure. I recommend using blunt tapestry needles for any kind of grafting or duplicate stitching.

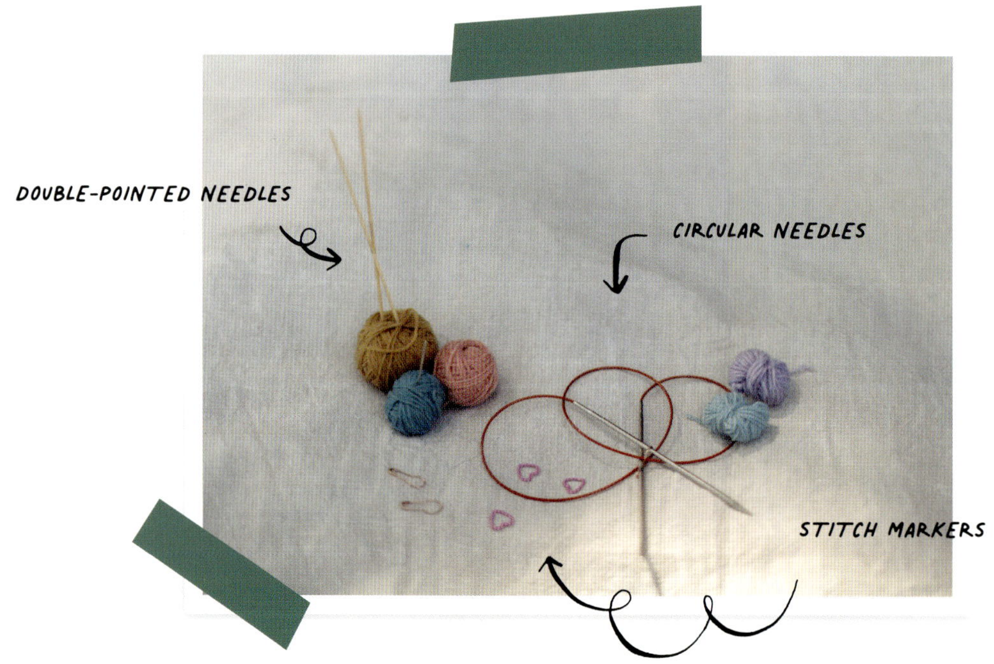

WESSEM SOCKS IN SCHEEPJES
METROPOLIS MARRAKECH 051
AND KRAKÓW 064

Chapter 2

CHOOSING COLOURS

Coming up with a colour palette can be the most delightful aspect of your knitting project, although it can be very daunting at the same time. Choosing the right colours is so important, because you want your motif to stand out as a reward for all your hard work. If there is little contrast between your two colours your motif might not be as visible, which would be a pity.

How do you find out if your colour combination has enough contrast? Nowadays it's very easy to set up a black-and-white filter on your phone camera, which is super helpful to check the contrast between colours. Make sure you have enough daylight and there are no harsh shadows, then look at your yarn through your camera lens. If you can clearly tell your yarns apart in greyscale, you can use them together for a colourwork motif.

If you are new to colourwork knitting, you can choose safe colour combinations such as white combined with a dark colour, or black with a light colour. If you don't feel comfortable choosing your own palette yet, feel free to use the exact colour combinations from the patterns. Throughout the book you will also see alternate colour options to inspire you.

Chapter 3

TENSION AND GAUGE

TENSION AND GAUGE

The dimensions of your knitted piece depend on your tension while knitting. Of course we want our knitted items to fit nicely, so it's definitely worth taking some time to check your tension.

In each pattern you will find the recommended tension for that project, and will for example be shown as '30 stitches and 30 rows of colourwork measure 10 x 10cm (4 x 4in). This means that horizontally you'll have 30 sts per 10cm (4in) of your work, and vertically 30 rows per 10cm (4in).

You can measure the tension on a knitted swatch, or on your actual project. For the projects in this book I actually recommend skipping the swatch and casting on your project right away. The advantage is that if your tension is similar to the recommended one, you can continue knitting your project. Another benefit is that for most projects you can try it on for size. The socks are knitted from the toe up, for instance, and you can easily try them on to see if you're knitting the right size.

If you work a tension swatch, make sure you're knitting in exactly the same way as you would for the actual project. All patterns in this book are knitted in the round, so you would knit your tension swatch in the round as well. Tension is measured over stranded colourwork, so make sure you knit a swatch with stranded colourwork and not just with one colour. Knitting a swatch can also be very helpful for trying out a new colour combination!

What to do if your tension does not match the pattern?
In our example of 30 stitches and 30 rows per 10 x 10cm (or 4 x 4in), let's look at the stitch tension. If you have more than 30 stitches per 10cm (4in), your stitches are narrower; this means you knit tighter so try a larger needle size. If you have less than 30 stitches per 10cm (4in), your stitches are wider which means you knit looser. You can correct this by using a smaller needle size. The same principle goes for row tension.

Sometimes it can be very tricky to get the correct stitch tension as well as the correct row temsion. What to do? In this case, I recommend using the needle size that gives you the right stitch tension. A difference in row tension can also be solved by knitting fewer or more rows than the pattern says. If, for example, you have 30 stitches per 10cm (4in), but 34 rows per 10cm (4in)? This means your rows are shorter, and you can choose to knit more rows than the pattern says. Another way to fix a tight tension is to stretch your project while damp. Please do note there's no way to undo this later.

When starting out with colourwork knitting it is very common that your tension is too loose or too tight. In most cases it helps to just keep practising. With each new project you will see an improvement in your tension because you will knit more and more relaxed. Keep trying and you'll improve in no time!

Chapter 4

READING PATTERNS

The patterns in this book are divided into several steps. First you'll see a list of materials including yarn and needle size. Then you'll find the recommended tension, the dimensions of your finished item, sizing information and a few knitting tips.

When a pattern has multiple sizes, you'll often see instructions for different sizes grouped together. The hat patterns are available in three sizes, which are shown as 1 (2) 3 in the pattern. If at the end of a round you see '100 (110) 120 sts', this means that you will have 100 stitches if you're knitting the first size, 110 stitches for the second size, and 120 stitches for the third size.

You will also see this in the amounts of yarn listed in the materials. If it reads that for Colour A you need '1 (1) 2 balls', you only need one ball for the first two sizes but you will need two balls for the third size.

The patterns in this book also use abbreviations to make them more compact – see Abbreviations and Techniques: Abbreviations. I recommend reading through Abbreviations and Techniques: Stranded Colourwork Knitting to help you to understand the colour charts.

Chapter 5

PATTERNS

Tip

The colourwork motifs have different skill levels. Choose motifs Wessem, Haelen or Leiden for an easier project, and Heerlen or Urmond for more challenging projects.

hats

The patterns in this book are sorted from easiest to most challenging.

Hats are great knitting projects to learn new techniques because they can be done relatively quickly. Even as a beginner knitter, you can knit a hat and get a taste for stranded colourwork knitting.

These hats are knitted from the brim up to the crown. You start with smaller needles for the ribbing and use the magic loop technique. If you have never knitted magic loop style before you can make it easier for yourself by choosing a circular needle 40cm (16in) long. This way you can concentrate on stranded colourwork knitting first before adding magic loop knitting into the mix.

WESSEM

· hat ·

MATERIALS

Scheepjes Metropolis
(200m/50g: 75% Extrafine Merino, 25% Nylon)

- Colour A: Seoul 035 × 1 (1) 1 ball
- Colour B: Philadelphia 007 × 1 (1) 1 ball

Recommended needle size for circular or double-pointed needles

- 2.25-2.5mm (US 1-1.5) for ribbing
- 3-3.25mm (US 2.5-3) for the rest

Recommended length circular needle

- 80cm (32in) for magic loop

Other materials

- Scissors
- Darning needle

TENSION

30 sts and 32 rounds of the stranded colourwork pattern on 3-3.25mm (US 2.5-3) needles measure 10×10cm (4×4in). If you have fewer sts per 10cm (4in) use a smaller needle size. If you have more sts per 10cm (4in) use a bigger needle size.

SIZES & MEASUREMENTS

This pattern is written for three adult sizes, the middle size fits most adults.

Size	**Head circumference**
Small	54-57cm (21-22½in)
Medium	58-60cm (23-24½in)
Large	60-63cm (24½-25in)

Instructions for different sizes are mentioned in the pattern as 'small (medium) large'.

WESSEM COWL

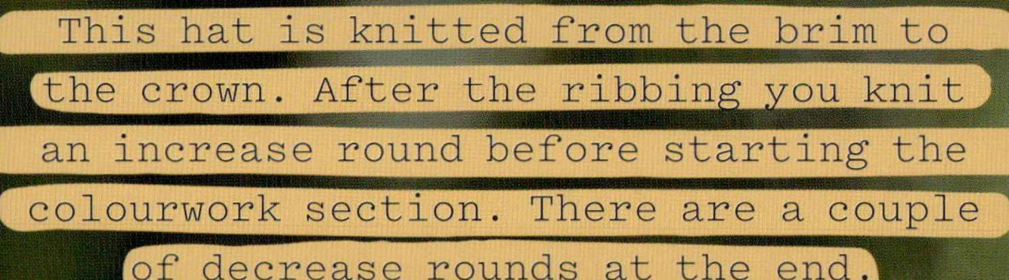
This hat is knitted from the brim to the crown. After the ribbing you knit an increase round before starting the colourwork section. There are a couple of decrease rounds at the end.

ALTERNATE COLOURWAY USES LIVERPOOL 065, SEOUL 035, TOULOUSE 030 AND PHILADELPHIA 007.

PATTERN

Start with 2.25mm or 2.5mm (US 1 or 1.5) needles for the brim. Using Colour A cast on 108 (120) 132 sts with the German Twisted Cast On (see Casting On and Off: German Twisted Cast On).
Knit the first 2 rows flat:

Rows 1-2
*K2, p2; rep from * to end.
Continue in the round.

Rounds 3-40
*K2, p2; rep from * to end.

Switch to 3mm or 3.25mm (US 2.5 or 3) needles.

Increase round
*K2, kfb; rep from * to end. [144 (160) 176 sts]

Next round
K all sts.

From the next round onwards you knit using Colours A and B. Start at Round 1 of Chart 1. Knit 42 rounds following Chart 1, that's 14 chart repeats in total.

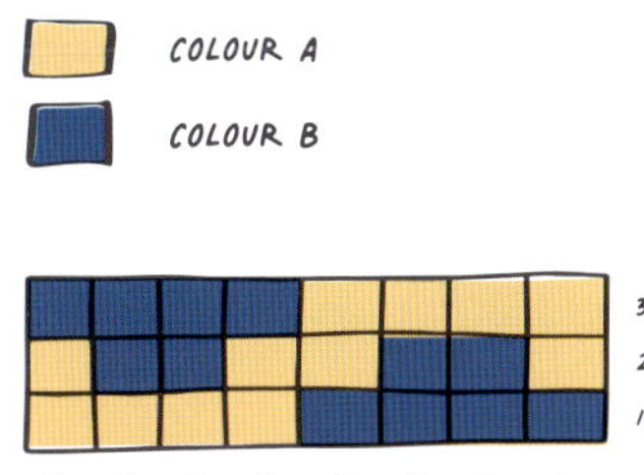

Chart 1

Read the chart from right to left and bottom to top. Each square counts as one stitch and the entire chart counts as one repeat of the pattern.

Continue with Chart 2 and the following instructions. The letter A or B is added after each instruction to refer to the yarn colour.

Crown round 1 (dec)
*K4B, k1A, k2togA, k1A; rep from * to end. [126 (140) 154 sts]

Crown round 2
*K1A, k2B, k4A; rep from * to end.

You can now cut Colour B. You've reached the end of Chart 2, continue as follows using Colour A only.

Crown round 3 (dec)
*K5, k2tog; rep from * to end. [108 (120) 132 sts]

Crown round 4
K all sts.

Crown round 5 (dec)
*K4, k2tog; rep from * to end. [90 (100) 110 sts]

Crown round 6
K all sts.

Crown round 7 (dec)
*K3, k2tog; rep from * to end. [72 (80) 88 sts]

Crown round 8
K all sts.

Crown round 9 (dec)
*K2, k2tog; rep from * to end. [54 (60) 66 sts]

Crown round 10
K all sts.

Crown round 11 (dec)
*K1, k2tog; rep from * to end. [36 (40) 44 sts]

Crown round 12
K all sts.

Crown round 13 (dec)
*K2tog; rep from * to end. [18 (20) 22 sts]

Cut yarn leaving a tail of 20cm (8in), weave the tail through all sts and pull tight.

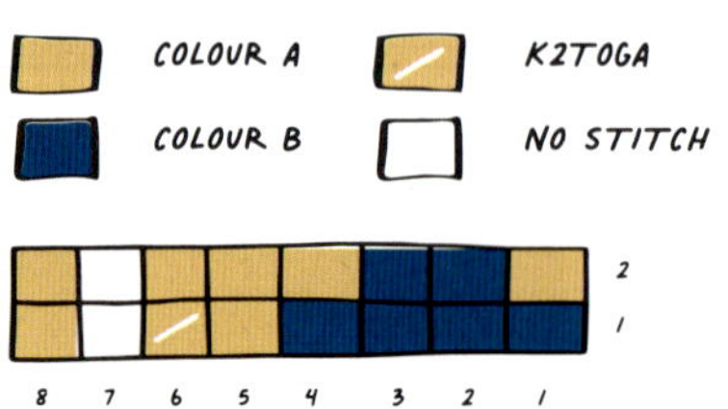

Chart 2

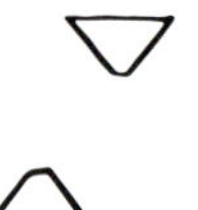

FINISHING

Weave in all ends. Please note: if you wear your hat with a folded brim, the reverse side will actually be on the outside. Weave the cast-on tail in on the right side to hide it from view.

Wash your hat by hand with a bit of wool detergent and squeeze any excess water out with a towel. Don't leave your hat to dry flat, but on something round like a balloon. Alternatively, put a bowl upside down on top of a vase and drape your hat over the top. Take care not to overstretch the brim. See more instructions in Abbreviations and Techniques: Washing and Blocking.

HAELEN
hat

MATERIALS

Scheepjes Metropolis
(200m/50g: 75% Extrafine Merino, 25% Nylon)

- Colour A: Depok 026 × 1 (1) 1 ball
- Colour B: Dubai 047 × 1 (1) 1 ball
- Colour C: Tokyo 061 × 1 (1) 1 ball

Recommended needle size for circular or double-pointed needles

- 2.25-2.5mm (US 1-1.5) for ribbing
- 3-3.25mm (US 2.5-3) for the rest

Recommended length circular needle

- 80cm (32in) for magic loop

Other materials

- Scissors
- Darning needle

TENSION

30 sts and 32 rounds of the stranded colourwork pattern on 3-3.25mm (US 2.5-3) needles measure 10×10cm (4×4in). If you have fewer sts per 10cm (4in) use a smaller needle size. If you have more sts per 10cm (4in) use a bigger needle size.

SIZES & MEASUREMENTS

This pattern is written for three adult sizes, the middle size fits most adults.

Size	Head circumference
Small	54-57cm (21-22½in)
Medium	58-60cm (23-24½in)
Large	60-63cm (24½-25in)

Instructions for different sizes are mentioned in the pattern as 'small (medium) large'.

This hat is knitted from the brim to the crown. After the ribbing you knit an increase round before starting the colourwork section. There are a couple of decrease rounds at the end.

PATTERN

Start with 2.25mm or 2.5mm (US 1 or 1.5) needles for the brim. Using Colour A cast on 112 (124) 136 sts with the German Twisted Cast On (see Casting On and Off: German Twisted Cast On).
Knit the first 2 rows flat:

Rows 1-2
*K2, p2; rep from * to end.

Rounds 3-40
*K2, p2; rep from * to end.

Switch to 3mm or 3.25mm (US 2.5 or 3) needles.

Increase round

- Size small: (k1, kfb) 7 times, (k2, kfb) 28 times - i.e. to last 14 sts- (k1, kfb) 7 times. [154 sts]
- Size medium: (k1, kfb) 4 times, (k2, kfb) 36 times - i.e. to last 8 sts- (k1, kfb) 4 times. [168 sts]
- Size large: K1, kfb, (k2, kfb) 44 times -i.e. to last 2 sts- k1, kfb. [182 sts]

Next round
K all sts.

From the next round onwards you knit using Colours A and B, and later you will add Colour C. Start at Round 1 of Chart 1. Knit 42 rounds following Chart 1, that's 3 chart repeats in total.

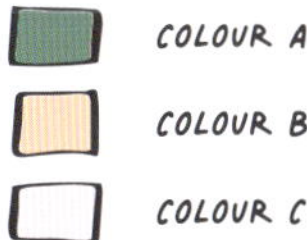

Read the chart from right to left and bottom to top. Each square counts as one stitch and the entire chart counts as one repeat of the pattern.

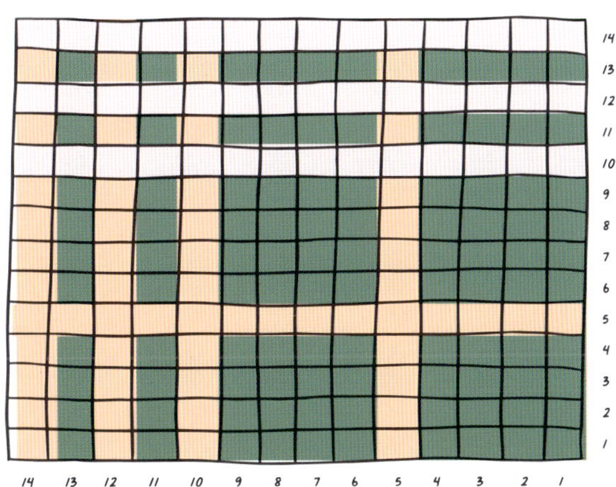

Chart 1

Cut Yarn C. Continue with Chart 2 and the following instructions. The letter A or B is added after each instruction to refer to the Colour A or B.

Crown round 1

*(K4A, k1B) 2 times, (k1A, k1B) 2 times; rep from * to end.

Crown round 2 (dec)

*(K2A, k2togA, k1B) 2 times, (k1A, k1B) 2 times; rep from * to end. [132 (144) 156 sts]

Crown rounds 3-4

*(K3A, k1B) 2 times, (k1A, k1B) 2 times; rep from * to end.

Crown round 5

K all sts using Colour B.

Crown round 6

*(K3A, k1B) 2 times, (k1A, k1B) 2 times; rep from *to end.

Crown round 7 (dec)

*(K1A, k2togA, k1B) 2 times, (k1A, k1B) 2 times; rep from * to end. [110 (120) 130 sts]

Crown rounds 8-9

*(K2A, k1B) 2 times, (k1A, k1B) 2 times; rep from * to end.

You can now cut Colour B. You've reached the end of Chart 2, continue as follows using Colour A only.

Crown round 10 (dec)

*K3, k2tog; rep from * to end. [88 (96) 104 sts]

Crown round 11

K all sts.

Crown round 12 (dec)

*K2, k2tog; rep from * to end. [66 (72) 78 sts]

Crown round 13

K all sts.

Crown round 14 (dec)

*K1, k2tog; rep from * to end. [44 (48) 52 sts]

Crown round 15 (dec)

*K2tog; rep from * to end. [22 (24) 26 sts]

Crown round 16 (dec)

*K2tog; rep from * to end. [11 (12) 13 sts]

Cut yarn leaving a tail of 20cm (8in), weave the tail through all sts and pull tight.

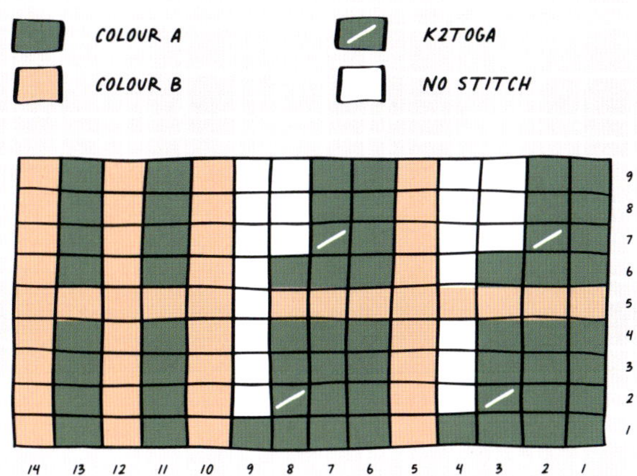

FINISHING

Weave in all ends. Please note: if you wear your hat with a folded brim, the reverse side will actually be on the outside. Weave the cast-on tail in on the right side to hide it from view.

Wash your hat by hand with a bit of wool detergent and squeeze any excess water out with a towel. Don't leave your hat to dry flat, but on something round like a balloon. Alternatively, put a bowl upside down on top of a vase and drape your hat over the top. Take care not to overstretch the brim. See more instructions in Abbreviations and Techniques: Washing and Blocking.

LEIDEN

hat

MATERIALS

Scheepjes Metropolis
(200m/50g: 75% Extrafine Merino, 25% Nylon)

- Colour A: Liverpool 065 × 1 (2) 2 balls
- Colour B: Marseille x 1 (1) 1 ball

Recommended needle size for circular or double-pointed needles

- 2.25-2.5mm (US 1-1.5) for ribbing
- 3-3.25mm (US 2.5-3) for the rest

Recommended length circular needle

- 80cm (32in) for magic loop

Other materials

- Scissors
- Darning needle

TENSION

30 sts and 32 rounds of the stranded colourwork pattern on 3-3.25mm (US 2.5-3) needles measure 10×10cm (4×4in). If you have fewer sts per 10cm (4in) use a smaller needle size. If you have more sts per 10cm (4in) use a bigger needle size.

SIZES & MEASUREMENTS

This pattern is written for three adult sizes, the middle size fits most adults.

Size	Head circumference
Small	54-57cm (21-22½in)
Medium	58-60cm (23-24½in)
Large	60-63cm (24½-25in)

Instructions for different sizes are mentioned in the pattern as 'small (medium) large'.

LEIDEN MITTENS

This hat is knitted from the brim to the crown. After the ribbing you knit an increase round before starting the colourwork section. There are a couple of decrease rounds at the end.

PATTERN

Start with 2.25mm or 2.5mm (US 1 or 1.5) needles for the brim. Using Colour A cast on 108 (120) 132 sts with the German Twisted Cast On (see Casting On and Off: German Twisted Cast On).
Knit the first 2 rows flat:

Rows 1-2
*K2, p2; rep from * to end.
Continue in the round.

Rounds 3-40
*K2, p2; rep from * to end.

Switch to 3mm or 3.25mm (US 2.5 or 3) needles.

Increase round
*K2, kfb; rep from * to end. [144 (160) 176 sts]

Next round
K all sts.

From the next round onwards you knit using Colours A and B. Start at Round 1 of Chart 1. Knit 40 rounds following Chart 1, that's 4 repeats of Rounds 1-10.

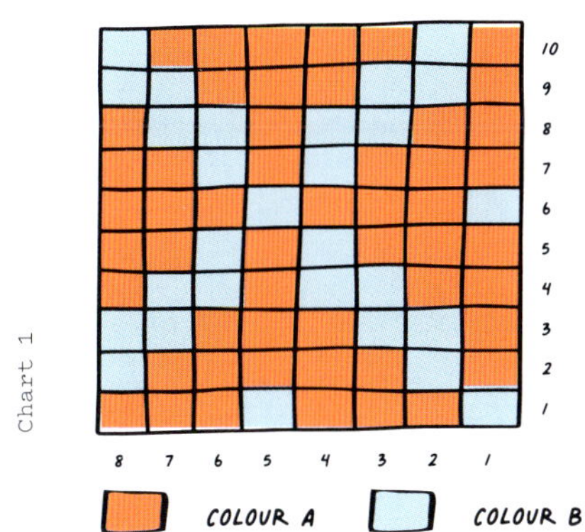

Read the chart from right to left and bottom to top.
Each square counts as one stitch and the entire chart counts as one repeat of the pattern.

Continue with Chart 2 and the following instructions. The letter A or B is added after each instruction to refer to the Colour A or B.

Crown round 1 (dec)
*K1B, k2A, k2togA, k3A; rep from * to end. [126 (140) 154 sts]

Crown round 2
*K1A, k1B, k4A, k1B; rep from * to end.

Crown round 3 (dec)
*K1A, k1B, k1A, k2togA, k1A, k1B; rep from * to end. [108 (120) 132 sts]

Crown round 4
*K1A, k2B; rep from * to end.

Crown round 5
*K2A, k1B, k1A, k1B, k1A; rep from * to end.

Crown round 6
*K3A, k1B, k2A; rep from * to end.

You can now cut Colour B. You've reached the end of Chart 2, continue as follows using Colour A only.

Crown round 7 (dec)
*K4, k2tog; rep from * to end. [90 (100) 110 sts]

Crown round 8
K all sts.

Crown round 9 (dec)
*K3, k2tog; rep from * to end. [72 (80) 88 sts]

Crown round 10
K all sts.

Crown round 11 (dec)
*K2, k2tog; rep from * to end. [54 (60) 66 sts]

Crown round 12
K all sts.

Crown round 13 (dec)
*K1, k2tog; rep from * to end. [36 (40) 44 sts]

Crown round 14 (dec)
*K2tog; rep from * to end. [18 (20) 22 sts]

Cut yarn leaving a tail of 20cm (8in), weave the tail through all sts and pull tight.

FINISHING

Weave in all ends. Please note: if you wear your hat with a folded brim, the reverse side will actually be on the outside. Weave the cast-on tail in on the right side to hide it from view.

Wash your hat by hand with a bit of wool detergent and squeeze any excess water out with a towel. Don't leave your hat to dry flat, but on something round like a balloon. Alternatively, put a bowl upside down on top of a vase and drape your hat over the top. Take care not to overstretch the brim. See more instructions in Abbreviations and Techniques: Washing and Blocking.

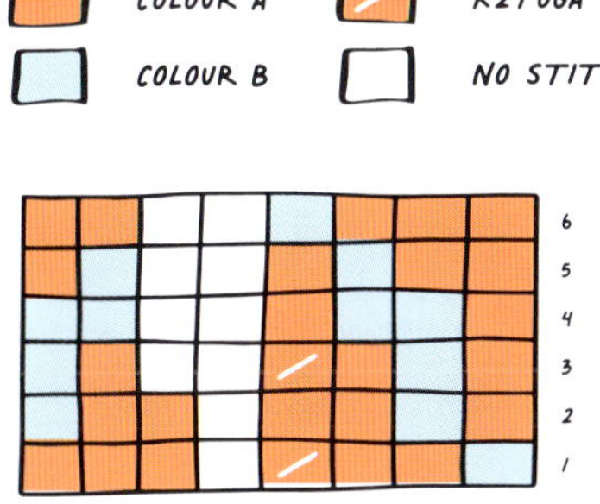

Chart 2

HEERLEN
· hat ·

MATERIALS

Scheepjes Metropolis
200m/50g: 75% Extrafine Merino, 25% Nylon)

- Colour A: Tokyo 061 × 1 (1) 1 ball
- Colour B: Dubai 047 × 1 (1) 1 ball
- Colour C: Philadelphia 007 x 1 (1) 1 ball

Recommended needle size for circular or double-pointed needles

- 2.25-2.5mm (US 1-1.5) for ribbing
- 3-3.25mm (US 2.5-3) for the rest

Recommended length circular needle

- 80cm (32in) for magic loop

Other materials

- Scissors
- Darning needle

TENSION

30 sts and 32 rounds of the stranded colourwork pattern on 3-3.25mm (US 2.5-3) needles measure 10×10cm (4×4in). If you have fewer sts per 10cm (4in) use a smaller needle size. If you have more sts per 10cm (4in) use a bigger needle size.

SIZES & MEASUREMENTS

This pattern is written for three adult sizes, the middle size fits most adults.

Size	Head circumference
Small	54-57cm (21-22½in)
Medium	58-60cm (23-24½in)
Large	60-63cm (24½-25in)

Instructions for different sizes are mentioned in the pattern as 'small (medium) large'.

This hat is knitted from the brim to the crown. After the ribbing you knit an increase round before starting the colourwork section. There are a couple of decrease rounds at the end.

PATTERN

Start with 2.25mm or 2.5mm (US 1 or 1.5) needles for the brim. Using Colour A cast on 104 (120) 134 sts with the German Twisted Cast On (see Casting On and Off: German Twisted Cast On).
Knit the first 2 rows flat:

Rows 1-2
*K2, p2; rep from * to end.
Continue in the round.

Rounds 3-40
*K2, p2; rep from * to end.

Switch to 3mm or 3.25mm (US 2.5 or 3) needles.

Increase round
Size small: k1, kfb, *k2, kfb; rep from * to end. [140 sts]
Size medium: *k2, kfb; rep from * to end [160 sts]
Size large: k1, kfb, *k2, kfb; rep from * to end [180 sts]

Next round
K all sts.

Cut Colour A. From the next round onwards you knit using Colours B and C. Start at Round 1 of Chart 1. Knit 40 rounds following Chart 1, that's ten repeats of Rounds 1-4 in total.

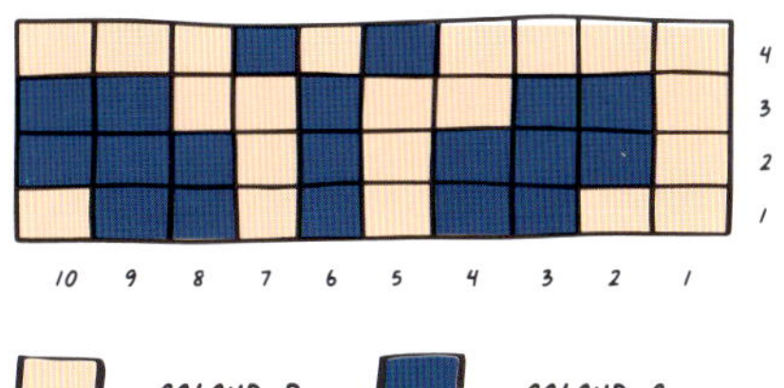

Read the chart from right to left and bottom to top. Each square counts as one stitch and the entire chart counts as one repeat of the pattern.

Chart 1

Continue with Chart 2 and the following instructions. The letter B or C is added after each instruction to refer to the Colour B or C.

Please note: the colour C stitch in Round 1 should line up with the stem from Chart 1.

Crown round 1 (dec)
*K2B, sskB, k1B, k1C, k1B, k2togB, k1B; rep from * to end. [112 (128) 144 sts].

Crown round 2
*K1C, k7B; rep from * to end.

Crown round 3
*K1B, k1C, k5B, k1C; rep from * to end.

Crown round 4
*K1C, k7B; rep from * to end.

You can now cut Colour C. You've reached the end of Chart 2, continue as follows using Colour B only.

Crown round 5 (dec)
*K2, k2tog; rep from * to end. [84 (96) 108 sts]

Crown round 6
K all sts.

Crown round 7 (dec)
*K1, k2tog; rep from * to end. [56 (64) 72 sts]

Crown round 8
K all sts.

Crown round 9 (dec)
*K2tog; rep from * to end. [28 (32) 36 sts]

Crown round 10
K all sts.

Crown round 11 (dec)
*K2tog; rep from * to end. [14 (16) 18 sts]

Cut yarn leaving a tail of 20cm (8in), weave the tail through all sts and pull tight.

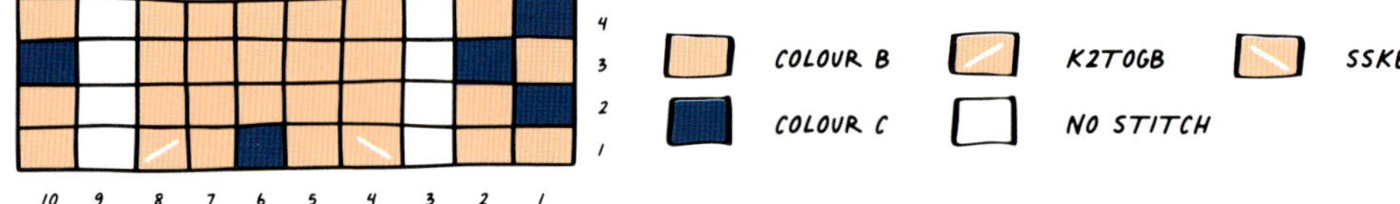

Chart 2

HAELEN MITTENS

ALTERNATE COLOURWAY MADE WITH CANBERRA 031, MONTERREY 023 AND MANILA 012.

FINISHING

Weave in all ends. Please note: if you wear your hat with a folded brim, the reverse side will actually be on the outside. Weave the cast-on tail in on the right side to hide it from view.

Wash your hat by hand with a bit of wool detergent and squeeze any excess water out with a towel. Don't leave your hat to dry flat, but on something round like a balloon. Alternatively, put a bowl upside down on top of a vase and drape your hat over the top. Take care not to overstretch the brim. See more instructions in Abbreviations and Techniques: Washing and Blocking.

URMOND
· hat ·

MATERIALS

Scheepjes Metropolis

200m/50g: 75% Extrafine Merino, 25% Nylon)

- Colour A: Bogotá 050 × 1 (2) 2 balls
- Colour B: Tokyo 061 × 1 (1) 1 ball

Recommended needle size for circular or double-pointed needles

- 2.25-2.5mm (US 1-1.5) for ribbing
- 3-3.25mm (US 2.5-3) for the rest

Recommended length circular needle

- 80cm (32in) for magic loop

Other materials

- Scissors
- Darning needle

TENSION

30 sts and 32 rounds of the stranded colourwork pattern on 3-3.25mm (US 2.5-3) needles measure 10×10cm (4×4in). If you have fewer sts per 10cm (4in) use a smaller needle size. If you have more sts per 10cm (4in) use a bigger needle size.

SIZES & MEASUREMENTS

This pattern is written for three adult sizes, the middle size fits most adults.

Size	**Head circumference**
Small	54-57cm (21-22½in)
Medium	58-60cm (23-24½in)
Large	60-63cm (24½-25in)

Instructions for different sizes are mentioned in the pattern as 'small (medium) large'.

URMOND COWL

This hat is knitted from the brim to the crown. After the ribbing you knit an increase round before starting the colourwork section. There are a couple of decrease rounds at the end.

PATTERN

Start with 2.25mm or 2.5mm (US 1 or 1.5) needles for the brim. Using Colour A cast on 108 (120) 132 sts with the German Twisted Cast On (see Casting On and Off: German Twisted Cast On).

Knit the first 2 rows flat:

Rows 1-2

*K2, p2; rep from * to end.

Continue in the round.

Rounds 3-40

*K2, p2; rep from * to end.

Switch to 3mm or 3.25mm (US 2.5 or 3) needles.

Increase round

*K2, kfb; rep from * to end. [144 (160) 176 sts]

Next round

K all sts.

From the next round onwards you knit using Colours A and B. Start at Round 1 of Chart 1. Knit 47 rounds following Chart 1, that's 2 repeats of Rounds 1-22, plus 1 repeat of Rounds 1-3.

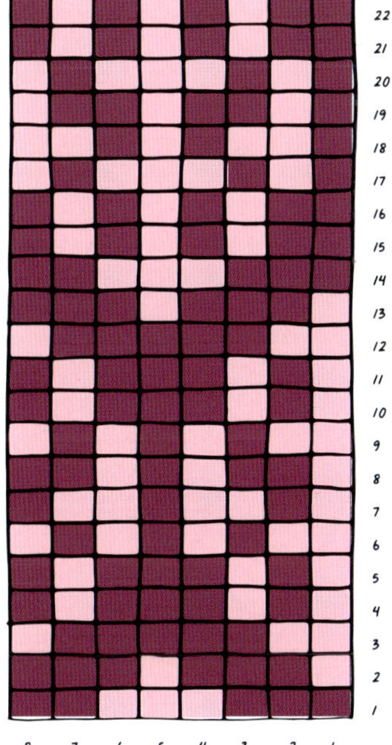

Chart 1

Read the chart from right to left and bottom to top. Each square counts as one stitch and the entire chart counts as one repeat of the pattern.

Continue with Chart 2 and the following instructions. The letter A or B is added after each instruction to refer to the Colour A or B.

Crown round 1 (dec)
*K1B, k1A, k1B, k2togA, k1A, k1B, k1A; rep from * to end. [126 (140) 154 sts]

Crown round 2
*K1B, k1A, k1B, k2A, k1B, k1A; rep from * to end.

Crown round 3 (dec)
*K1B, k1A, k1B, k2togA, k1B, k1A; rep from * to end. [108 (120) 132 sts]

Crown round 4
*K2B, k3A, k1B; rep from * to end.

Crown round 5 (dec)
*K1B, k2A, k2togA, k1A; rep from * to end. [90 (100) 110 sts]

You can now cut Colour B. You've reached the end of Chart 2, continue as follows using Colour A only.

Crown round 6
K all sts.

Crown round 7 (dec)
*K3, k2tog; rep from * to end. [72 (80) 88 sts]

Crown round 8
K all sts.

Crown round 9 (dec)
*K2, k2tog; rep from * to end. [54 (60) 66 sts]

Crown round 10
K all sts.

Crown round 11 (dec)
*K1, k2tog; rep from * to end. [36 (40) 44 sts]

Crown round 12 (dec)
*K2tog; rep from * to end. [18 (20) 22 sts]

Cut yarn leaving a tail of 20cm (8in), weave the tail through all sts and pull tight.

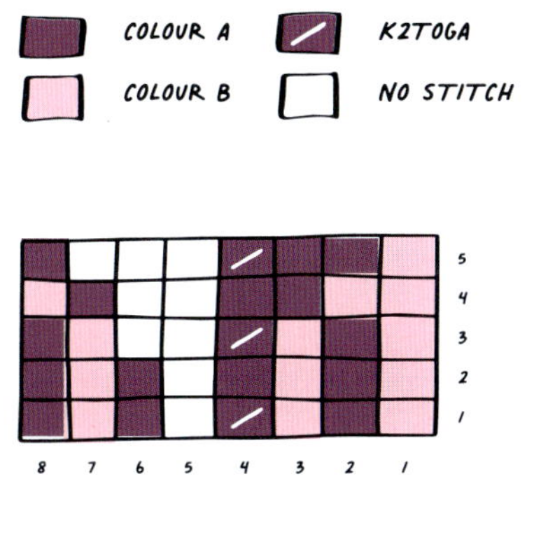

Chart 2

FINISHING

Weave in all ends. Please note: if you wear your hat with a folded brim, the reverse side will actually be on the outside. Weave the cast-on tail in on the right side to hide it from view.

Wash your hat by hand with a bit of wool detergent and squeeze any excess water out with a towel. Don't leave your hat to dry flat, but on something round like a balloon. Alternatively, put a bowl upside down on top of a vase and drape your hat over the top. Take care not to overstretch the brim. See more instructions in Abbreviations and Techniques: Washing and Blocking.

WESSEM COWL

LEIDEN COWL

HAELEN COWL

URMOND COWL

The Wessem and Urmond cowls have a colour change halfway through; of course you can choose to change colours with the other designs as well. Let your creativity run free and make your knitting project unique!

cowls

The cowls may be my favourite designs from this entire book, simply because they're so big! Stranded colourwork makes your knitted fabric twice as warm. Cowls are my go-to accessory for bike riding since they stay put and don't get caught in the wheels.

On the one hand, cowls are easier to knit than hats, for example, because there are no increases or decreases so you can knit the entire project on the same needle. On the other hand these cowls do require some perseverance as you'll need to spend quite a few hours knitting them.

The cowl designs in this book come in two different lengths. Make the shorter version if you want to wear it as a single layer around your neck. The longer version is made to loop around your neck twice, so you get double the warmth. The pictures show the shorter versions of the Wessem and Heerlen cowls, and the longer versions of the Haelen, Leiden and Urmond cowls.

WESSEM
· cowl ·

MATERIALS

Scheepjes Metropolis
(200m/50g: 75% Extrafine Merino, 25% Nylon)

- Colour A: Seoul 035 × 2 (3) balls
- Colour B: Philadelphia 007 × 1 (2) balls
- Colour C: Toulouse 030 × 1 (2) balls

Recommended needle size for circular or double-pointed needles

- 4mm (US 6)

Recommended length circular needle

- 40cm (16in)

Other materials

- Scissors
- Darning needle

TENSION

28 sts and 28 rounds of the stranded colourwork pattern on 4mm (US 6) needles measure 10×10cm (4×4in).

SIZES & MEASUREMENTS

You can knit this cowl in two different lengths: 60cm (23½in) and 120cm (47in). Wear the shorter version as a single loop, and the longer version as a double loop. With the recommended tension your cowl will be 21.5cm (8½in) wide.

WESSEM MITTENS

Knit this cowl in the round to form a long tube. Change colours halfway through to get a fun two-tone effect. At the end you'll be sewing the last round to the cast on round.

Read the chart from right to left and bottom to top. Each square counts as one stitch and the entire chart counts as one repeat of the pattern.

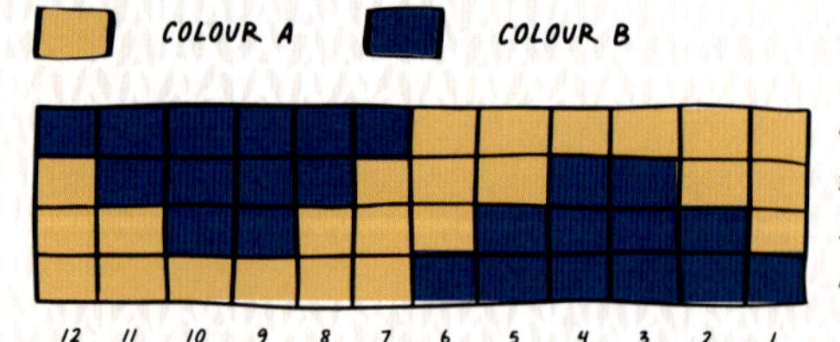

Chart 1

PATTERN

Using 4mm (US 6) needles and Colour A, cast on 120 sts with the longtail cast on – see Casting On and Off: Long Tail Cast On. Join in the round. From Round 1 onwards, join Colour B and start knitting from Chart 1. Choose whether you're making the shorter version of 60cm (23½in) or the longer version of 120cm (47in).

Shorter version

Knit 21 repeats of Chart 1 for a total of 84 rounds. Cut Colour B. From the next round start reading from Chart 2 where you'll be working with Colours A and C. Knit 21 repeats of Chart 2 so that you'll have worked a total of 168 rounds. Continue with the finishing instructions.

Longer version

Knit 42 repeats of Chart 1 for a total of 168 rounds. Cut Colour B. From the next round start reading from Chart 2 where you'll be working with Colours A and C. Knit 42 repeats from Chart 2 so that you'll have worked a total of 336 rounds. Continue with the finishing instructions.

FINISHING

Do not cast off yet. Cut Colour C. For Colour A, leave a tail of about 30cm (12in) before cutting it. Weave in all other ends except the Colour A tail.

Put the last round on waste yarn, wash your cowl and block it. See more instructions in Abbreviations and Techniques: Washing and Blocking.

When dry, put the last round back on a knitting needle. Lay your cowl onto a flat surface with the last round towards you and the cast on round facing away from you. Then fold both ends towards each other. Find the beginning of the round on both ends of your cowl and make sure your cowl is not twisted.

Using Half Mattress Stitch and Colour A tail, sew the live stitches of your last round to the cast-on round – see Casting On and Off: Half Mattress Stitch or watch the video via the QR code. Don't pull your yarn too tight while seaming.

After seaming all the way around, weave in your last end. The result is a nice almost invisible finish.

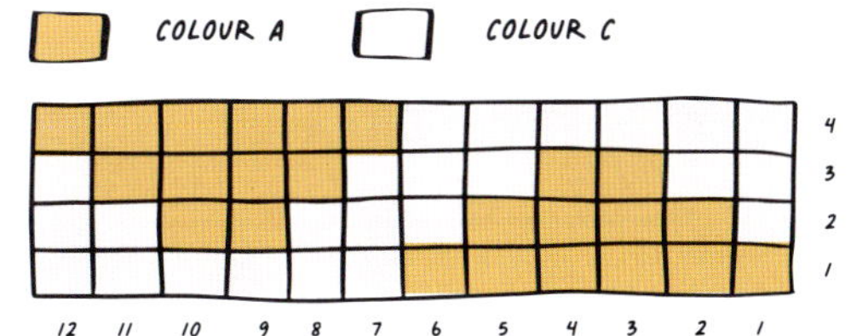

Chart 2

HAELEN
· cowl ·

MATERIALS

Scheepjes Metropolis
200m/50g: 75% Extrafine Merino, 25% Nylon)

- Colour A: Depok 026 × 2 (3) balls
- Colour B: Dubai 047 × 1 (2) balls
- Colour C: Tokyo 061 × 1 (2) balls

Tip

You'll need about 52 grams of Colour C for the longer version, you might be lucky enough to get that from one ball.

Recommended needle size for circular or double-pointed needles

- 4mm (US 6)

Recommended length circular needle

- 40cm (16in)

Other materials

- Scissors
- Darning needle

TENSION

28 sts and 28 rounds of the stranded colourwork pattern on 4mm (US 6) needles measure 10×10cm (4×4in).

SIZES & MEASUREMENTS

You can knit this cowl in two different lengths: 60cm (23½in) and 120cm (47in). Wear the shorter version as a single loop, and the longer version as a double loop. With the recommended tension your cowl will be 22.5cm (9in) wide.

HAELEN HAT

Knit this cowl in the round to form a long tube. At the end you'll be sewing the last round to the cast on round.

Read the chart from right to left and bottom to top.
Each square counts as one stitch and the entire chart counts as one repeat of the pattern.

PATTERN

Using 4mm (US 6) needles and Colour A, cast on 126 sts with the longtail cast on - see Casting On and Off: Long Tail Cast On. Join in the round. Join Colour B and start knitting Round 1 from Chart 1. When you get to Round 10, also join in Colour C. Choose whether you're making the shorter version of 60cm (23½in) or the longer version of 120cm (47in).

Shorter version

Knit 11 repeats of all Chart rounds plus a final repeat of Rounds 1-13 only for a total of 167 rounds. To be clear, do not knit Round 14 of the last repeat. Continue with the finishing instructions.

Longer version

Knit 23 repeats of all Chart rounds plus a final repeat of Rounds 1-13 only for a total of 335 rounds. To be clear, do not knit Round 14 of the last repeat. Continue with the finishing instructions.

14 13 12 11 10 9 8 7 6 5 4 3 2 1

14 13 12 11 10 9 8 7 6 5 4 3 2 1

Chart

FINISHING

Do not cast off yet. Cut Colours A and B. For Colour C, leave a tail of about 30cm (12in) before cutting it. Weave in all other ends except the Colour C tail.

Put the last round on waste yarn, wash your cowl and block it. See more instructions in Abbreviations and Techniques: Washing and Blocking.

When dry, put the last round back on a knitting needle. Lay your cowl onto a flat surface with the last round towards you and the cast-on round facing away from you. Then fold both ends towards each other. Find the beginning of the round on both ends of your cowl and make sure your cowl is not twisted.

Using Half Mattress Stitch and Colour C tail, sew the live stitches of your last round to the cast-on round - see Casting On and Off: Half Mattress Stitch or watch the video via the QR code. Don't pull your yarn too tight while seaming.

After seaming all the way around, weave in your last end. The result is a nice almost invisible finish.

COLOUR A

COLOUR B

COLOUR C

LEIDEN
cowl

MATERIALS

Scheepjes Metropolis
200m/50g: 75% Extrafine Merino, 25% Nylon)

- Colour A: Liverpool 065 × 2 (4) balls
- Colour B: Marseille 019 × 1 (2) balls

Recommended needle size for circular or double-pointed needles

- 4mm (US 6)

Recommended length circular needle

- 40cm (16in)

Other materials

- Scissors
- Darning needle

TENSION

28 sts and 28 rounds of the stranded colourwork pattern on 4mm (US 6) needles measure 10×10cm (4×4in).

SIZES & MEASUREMENTS

You can knit this cowl in two different lengths: 60cm (23½in) and 120cm (47in). Wear the shorter version as a single loop, and the longer version as a double loop. With the recommended tension your cowl will be 21.5cm (8½in) wide.

Knit this cowl in the round to form a long tube. At the end you'll be sewing the last round to the cast on round.

PATTERN

Using 4mm (US 6) needles and Colour A, cast on 120 sts with the longtail cast on - see Casting On and Off: Long Tail Cast On. Join in the round. Join in Colour B and start knitting from Round 1 of Chart 1. Choose whether you're making the shorter version of 60cm (23½in) or the longer version of 120cm (47in).

Shorter version
Knit 17 repeats of the Chart for a total of 170 rounds. Continue with the finishing instructions.

Longer version
Knit 34 repeats of the Chart for a total of 340 rounds. Continue with the finishing instructions.

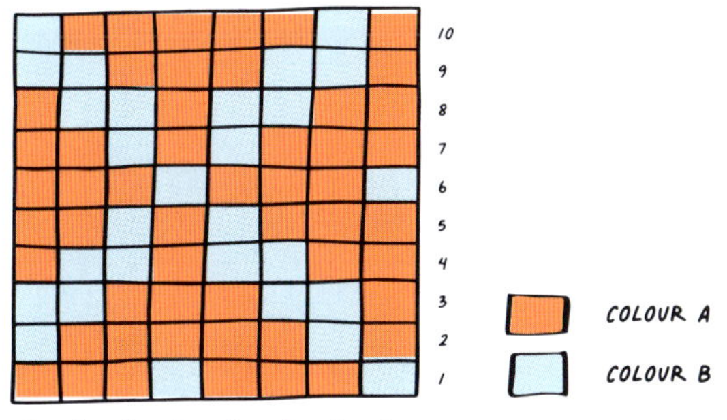

Read the chart from right to left and bottom to top. Each square counts as one stitch and the entire chart counts as one repeat of the pattern.

Chart

FINISHING

Do not cast off yet. Cut Colour B. For Colour A, leave a tail of about 30cm (12in) before cutting it. Weave in all other ends except the Colour A tail.

Put the last round on waste yarn, wash your cowl and block it. See more instructions in Abbreviations and Techniques: Washing and Blocking.

When dry, put the last round back on a knitting needle. Lay your cowl onto a flat surface with the last round towards you and the cast on round facing away from you. Then fold both ends towards each other. Find the beginning of the round on both ends of your cowl and make sure your cowl is not twisted.

Using Half Mattress Stitch and Colour A tail, sew the live stitches of your last round to the cast-on round - see Casting On and Off: Half Mattress Stitch or watch the video via the QR code. Don't pull your yarn too tight while seaming.

After seaming all the way around, weave in your last end. The result is a nice almost invisible finish.

HEERLEN
cowl

MATERIALS

Scheepjes Metropolis

200m/50g: 75% Extrafine Merino, 25% Nylon)

- Colour A: Dubai 047 × 2 (3) balls
- Colour B: Philadelphia 007 × 2 (3) balls

Recommended needle size for circular or double-pointed needles

- 4mm (US 6)

Recommended length circular needle

- 40cm (16in)

Other materials

- Scissors
- Darning needle

TENSION

28 sts and 28 rounds of the stranded colourwork pattern on 4mm (US 6) needles measure 10×10cm (4×4in).

SIZES & MEASUREMENTS

You can knit this cowl in two different lengths: 60cm (23½in) and 120cm (47in). Wear the shorter version as a single loop, and the longer version as a double loop. With the recommended tension your cowl will be 21.5cm (8½in) wide.

HEERLEN HAT

Knit this cowl in the round to
form a long tube. At the end
you'll be sewing the last round
to the cast on round.

PATTERN

Using 4mm (US 6) needles and Colour A, cast on 120 sts with the longtail cast on - see Casting On and Off: Long Tail Cast On. Join in the round. From Round 1 onwards, also take Colour B and start knitting from Chart 1. Choose whether you're making the shorter version of 60cm (23½in) or the longer version of 120cm (47in).

Shorter version
Knit 42 repeats of the Chart for a total of 168 rounds. Continue with the finishing instructions.

Longer version
Knit 84 repeats of the Chart for a total of 336 rounds. Continue with the finishing instructions.

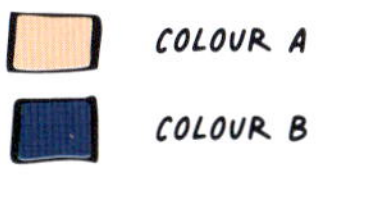

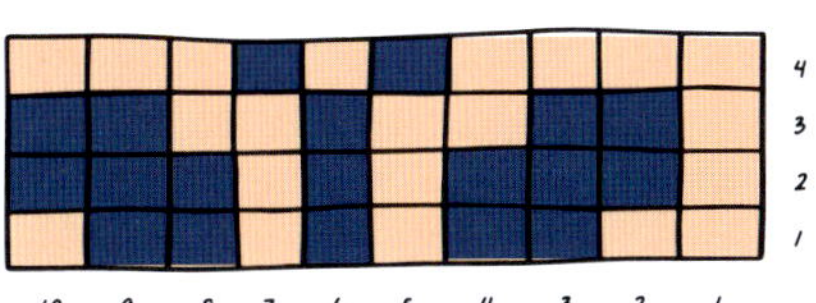

Read the chart from right to left and bottom to top. Each square counts as one stitch and the entire chart counts as one repeat of the pattern.

FINISHING

Do not cast off yet. Cut Colour B. For Colour A, leave a tail of about 30cm (12in) before cutting it. Weave in all other ends except the Colour A tail.

Put the last round on waste yarn, wash your cowl and block it. See more instructions in Abbreviations and Techniques: Washing and Blocking.

When dry, put the last round back on a knitting needle. Lay your cowl onto a flat surface with the last round towards you and the cast on round facing away from you. Then fold both ends towards each other. Find the beginning of the round on both ends of your cowl and make sure your cowl is not twisted.

Using Half Mattress Stitch and Colour A tail, sew the live stitches of your last round to the cast-on round - see Casting On and Off: Half Mattress Stitch or watch the video via the QR code. Don't pull your yarn too tight while seaming.

After seaming all the way around, weave in your last end. The result is a nice almost invisible finish.

URMOND
cowl

MATERIALS

Scheepjes Metropolis

200m/50g: 75% Extrafine Merino, 25% Nylon)

- Colour A: Bogotá 050 × 1 (2) balls
- Colour B: Tokyo 061 × 1 (2) balls
- Colour C: Depok 026 × 1 (2) balls
- Colour D: Suwon 018 × 1 (2) balls

Tip

For the longer version you'll need about 56 grams each of Colours B and D. You might be able to use leftovers instead of a new 2nd ball.

Recommended needle size for circular or double-pointed needles

- 4mm (US 6)

Recommended length circular needle

- 40cm (16in)

Other materials

- Scissors
- Darning needle

TENSION

28 sts and 28 rounds of the stranded colourwork pattern on 4mm (US 6) needles measure 10×10cm (4×4in).

SIZES & MEASUREMENTS

You can knit this cowl in two different lengths: 60cm (23½in) and 120cm (47in). Wear the shorter version as a single loop, and the longer version as a double loop. With the recommended tension your cowl will be 22.5cm (9in) wide.

URMOND HAT

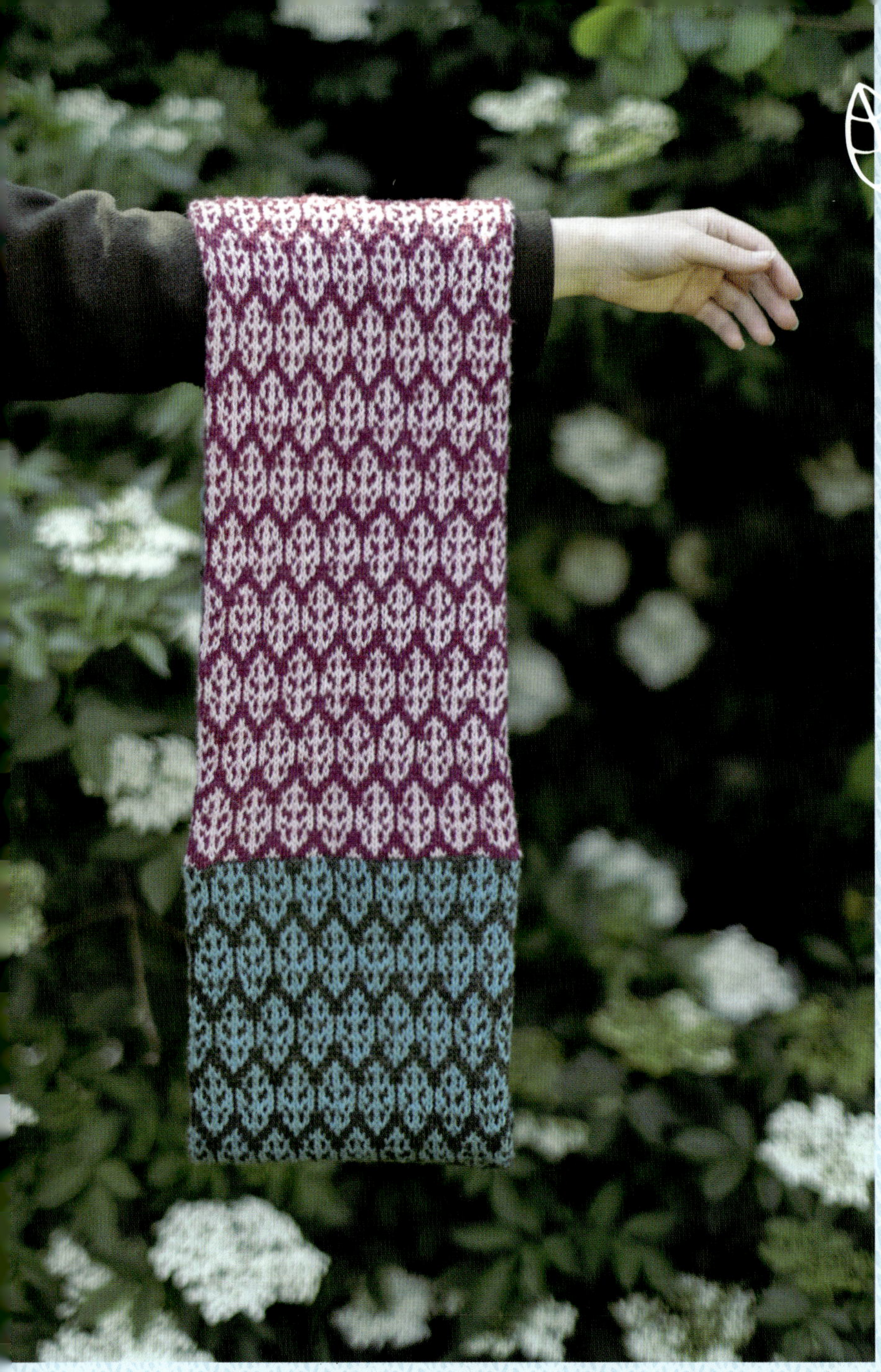

Knit this cowl in the round to form a long tube. Change colours halfway through to get a fun two-tone effect. At the end you'll be sewing the last round to the cast on round.

PATTERN

Using 4mm (US 6) needles and Colour A, cast on 128 sts with the longtail cast on - see Casting On and Off: Long Tail Cast On. Join in the round. Join Colour B and start knitting from Round 1 of Chart 1. Choose whether you're making the shorter version of 60cm (23½in) or the longer version of 120cm (47in).

Shorter version

Knit 4 repeats of Chart 1 for a total of 88 rounds. Cut Colours A and B. From the next round start reading from Chart 2 where you'll be working with Colours C and D. Knit 4 repeats of Chart 2 so that you'll have Worked a total of 176 rounds. Continue with the finishing instructions.

Longer version

Knit 8 repeats of Chart 1 for a total of 176 rounds. Cut Colours A and B. From the next round start reading from Chart 2 where you'll be working with Colours C and D. Knit 8 repeats from Chart 2 so that you'll have worked a total of 352 rounds. Continue with the finishing instructions.

FINISHING

Do not cast off yet. Cut Colour D. For Colour C, leave a tail of about 30cm (12in) before cutting it. Weave in all other ends except the Colour C tail.

Put the last round on waste yarn, wash your cowl and block it. See more instructions in Abbreviations and Techniques: Washing and Blocking.

When dry, put the last round back on a knitting needle. Lay your cowl onto a flat surface with the last round towards you and the cast on round facing away from you. Then fold both ends towards each other. Find the beginning of the round on both ends of your cowl and make sure your cowl is not twisted.

Using Half Mattress Stitch and Colour C tail, sew the live stitches of your last round to the cast-on round - see Casting On and Off: Half Mattress Stitch, or watch the video via the QR code. Don't pull your yarn too tight while seaming.

After seaming all the way around, weave in your last end. The result is a nice almost invisible finish.

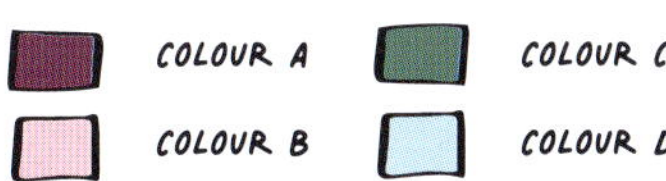

Read the chart from right to left and bottom to top. Each square counts as one stitch and the entire chart counts as one repeat of the pattern.

GENERAL INFORMATION

Measuring your hand

The pattern for the mittens comes in two widths, 18cm (7in) and 21cm (8in). This is the circumference of the knuckles. The mittens are pretty stretchy so this measurement does not have to be exact.

The length of your mittens can be customized. Measure from the inner corner of your thumb to the fingertips. The pattern is written for a standard length of 12cm (4¾in). If your measurement is shorter or longer, you can knit fewer rounds or add more rounds for the hand.

Knitting mittens

These mittens are knit from the cuff to the fingertips. Use smaller needles for the ribbing and solid colour sections, and bigger needles for the colourwork.

While knitting the hand in colourwork, you'll be increasing on one side for the thumb. Knit the thumb in just the background colour while you're stranding the pattern colour along on the inside of your work. See Abbreviations and Instructions: Stranded Colourwork Knitting.

After the thumb increases are done, the thumb stitches are placed onto waste yarn and you will continue knitting on the hand section.

Please note there are different instructions for the left and right mitten. The top of each mitten is closed with Kitchener stitch.

After finishing the hand section, return to the thumb stitches and finish knitting the thumb.

mittens

Mittens are quite the challenge to knit, because you're knitting colourwork and keeping track of your increases at the same time. You do get a lot of satisfaction from it in return. I remember when I knit my first mittens I thought: wow, I really made these!

If the idea of knitting mittens intimidates you, I invite you to knit them in one colour first, using the smaller needle size throughout. Forget about the colourwork and focus on the construction. Even without the colourwork motif they will match the rest of the set beautifully!

FOR ALL MITTENS

Start at the pattern page for the mittens you want to make, then come back to this page for the general information and common parts of the pattern.

MATERIALS

Recommended needle size for circular or double-pointed needles

- 2.25mm (US 1) for the cuff and solid colour sections
- 2.5mm (US 1.5) for the colourwork sections

Recommended length circular needle

- 80cm (32in) for magic loop

Other materials

- Waste yarn
- 2 stitch markers
- Scissors
- Darning Needle

SPECIAL ABBREVIATIONS

k1A - knit 1 stitch using Colour A
m1A - make 1 stitch using Colour A
k1B - knit 1 stitch using Colour B
m1B - make 1 stitch using Colour B

TENSION

33-34 sts and 35 rounds of the stranded colourwork pattern on 2.5mm (US 1.5) needles measure 10×10cm (4×4in).

SIZES & MEASUREMENTS

This pattern contains instructions for two sizes. Measure the hand circumference over the base knuckles. Instructions for different sizes are referred to in the pattern as: small (large).

Size	Hand circumference
Small	18cm (7in)
Large	21cm (8in)

THUMB

Put the 24 thumb sts on 2.25mm (US 1) needles.

Rounds 1-20
Knit all sts.
Round 21
K2tog to end. [12 sts]

Cut yarn with 10cm (4in) end. Thread yarn through all sts with darning needle, pull tight and weave in the end.

FINISHING

Please note: the Haelen mittens have specific finishing instructions noted in the pattern.

Use the cast-on tail of Colour A to seam the split in the cuff. For the thumb, use the Colour A tail at the base (Colour B for the Heerlen mittens) to sew the hole closed. Weave in all ends. Wash the mittens and lay flat to dry.

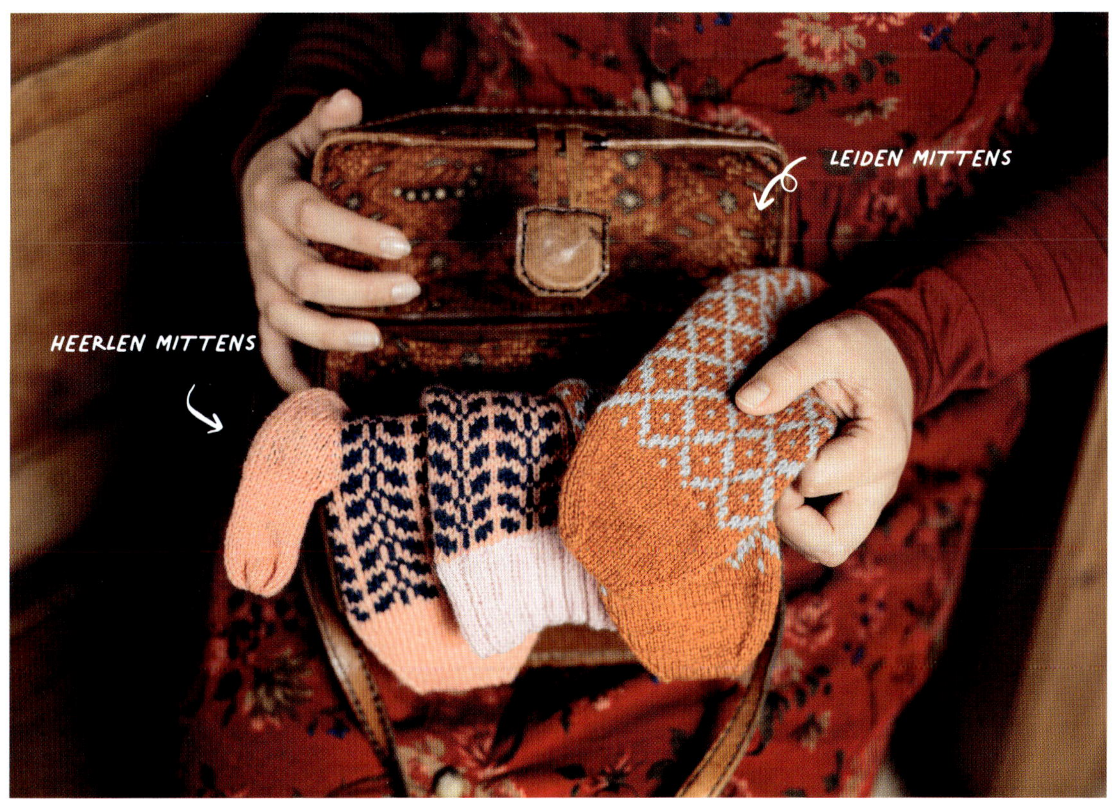

WESSEM
·mittens·

MATERIALS

Scheepjes Metropolis
(200m/50g: 75% Extrafine Merino, 25% Nylon)

- Colour A: Seoul 035 × 1 ball
- Colour B: Philadelphia 007 × 1 ball

Read the chart from right to left and bottom to top. Each square counts as one stitch and the entire chart counts as one repeat of the pattern.

The white squares in Chart 2 do not count as a stitch. Skip them and start the round at the first coloured square. Red lines mark the stitch marker placement.

COLOUR A

COLOUR B

M1 WITH COLOUR A

NO STITCH

STITCH MARKER

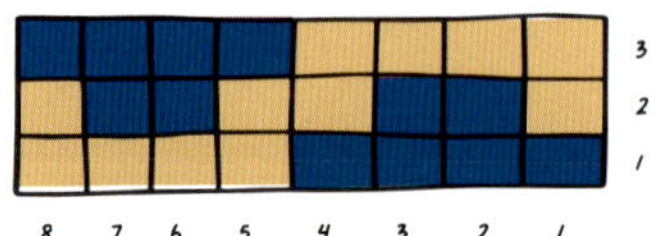

Chart 1

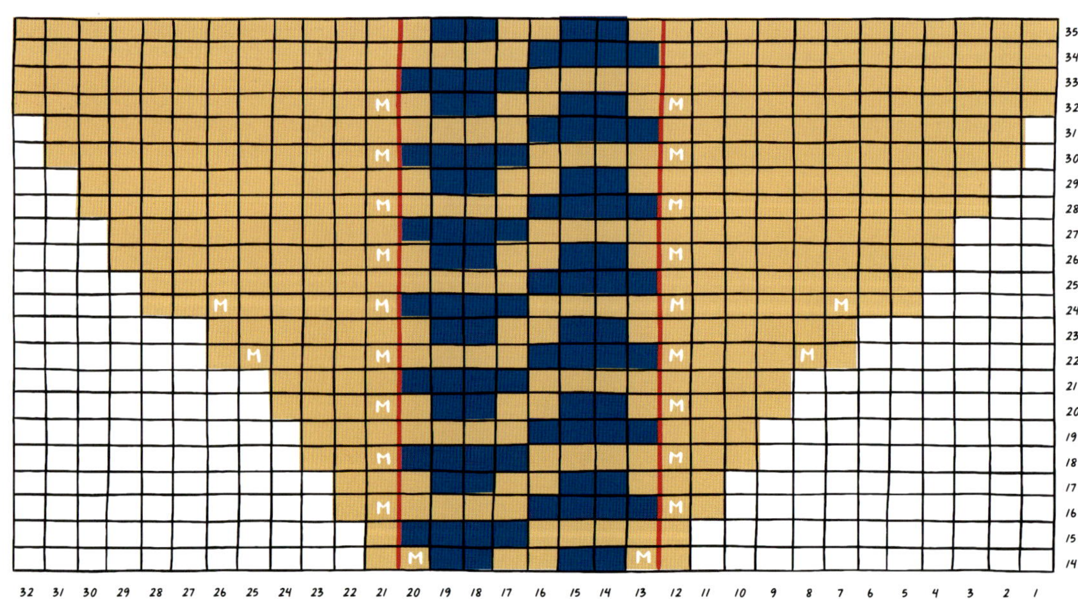

Chart 2 - thumb increases

PATTERN

Using Colour A and 2.25mm (US 1) needles, cast on 56 (64) sts with the German Twisted Cast On (see Casting On and Off: German Twisted Cast On).
Knit the first 2 rows flat:

Rows 1-2
*K2, p2; rep from * to end.
Continue knitting in the round.

Rounds 3-18
*K2, p2; rep from * to end.

Change to 2.5mm (US 1.5) needles.

Rounds 19-20
K all sts.

Join Colour B and start knitting from Chart 1. Knit 4 repeats of Chart 1, then knit Round 1 once more for a total of 13 rounds.

From the next round start increasing on one side for the thumb. Be sure to check Chart 2 as well as the instructions. In Round 14 you'll be placing two stitch markers. The stitches in between those two markers are to be knitted according to the repeat in Chart 1.

Increase round (Round 14)
K1A, pm, m1A. The m1-stitch now counts as the first stitch of the repeat shown in Chart 1. Knit according to Chart 1 until 1 st left, then: m1A, pm, k1A. The last m1-stitch now counts as the last stitch in the repeat. [2 sts inc]

The stitch markers now mark the beginning and end of the colourwork section. The stitches outside of the markers are your thumb sts as shown in Chart 2.

Straight round (odd numbered rounds)
K all sts using A to marker, sm, work colourwork patt to marker, sm, k using A to end.

Increase round (even numbered rounds)
K all sts using A until marker, m1A, sm, work colourwork patt to marker, sm, m1A, k using A to end.

Knit 1 round straight.

Repeat the increase round and straight round until you have increased 8 sts in total, 4 sts on either side of the colourwork section. Don't forget to knit the last straight round. [64 (72) sts]

Always pick up a Colour A strand for the M1 increase.

In the following 2 increase rounds you increase 4 sts per round instead of 2 sts.

Increase round (Round 22)
K1A, m1A, k3A, m1A, sm, work colourwork patt to marker, sm, m1A, k3A, m1A, k1A.

Knit 1 round straight.

Increase round (Round 24)
K2A, m1A, k4A, m1A, sm, work colourwork patt to marker, sm, m1A, k4A, m1A, k2A.

Knit 1 round straight.

For the following increase rounds you increase 2 sts per round again.

Increase round
K all sts using A until m, m1A, sm, work colourwork patt to marker, sm, m1A, k using A to end.

Knit 1 round straight.

Alternate between knitting an increase round and a straight round until you have increased 24 sts in total, 12 sts on either side of the colourwork section. [80 (88) sts]

After your last increase round knit 3 rounds straight in total. At this point you should have worked 11 whole repeats of the patt from Chart 1, plus 1 additional repeat of Rounds 1-2. In Chart 2 you have now reached the end of Round 35.

SPLIT FOR THE THUMB

Knit using A to marker, then put thumb sts on waste yarn. The thumb sts are the first 12 sts of the round and the last 12 sts of the round. Remove stitch markers.

Continue knitting according to Chart 1 over the remaining 56 (64) sts.

Put a clip or clothes pin on the thumb to avoid laddering at the start of the round.

Continue knitting until you've worked 19 repeats of Chart 1, which comes to 57 rounds.

Change to 2.25mm (US 1) needles.

Cut Colour B and continue using only Colour A.

Right mitten

Next round: K all sts until 6 sts left. This will be the new start of the round. From this point, divide your sts evenly in two halves of 28 (32) sts across your needles.

Left mitten

Next round: K 6 sts. This will be the new start of the round. From this point, divide your sts evenly in two halves of 28 (32) sts across your needles.

Both mittens

Next round: K all sts.
Check that each half has the same number of sts. You will decrease by 4 sts each decrease round.

Repeating pattern for decreases:

Round 1 (dec)

K1, ssk, k until last 3 sts of first half, k2tog, k1. Repeat for second half.

Rounds 2-4

K all sts.

Knit this repeat 3 times in total, you now have 44 (52) sts remaining.

Then:

Round 1 (dec)

K1, ssk, k until last 3 sts of first half, k2tog, k1. Repeat for second half.

Round 2

K all sts.
Knit this repeat 5 times in total, but omit the last straight round. You now have 24 (32) sts remaining.

There are 12 (16) sts on each needle. Seam closed with Kitchener stitch - see Casting On and Casting Off: Kitchener Stitch.

THUMB AND FINISHING INSTRUCTIONS

See For All Mittens: Finishing.

HAELEN
·mittens·

MATERIALS

Scheepjes Metropolis

(200m/50g: 75% Extrafine Merino, 25% Nylon)

- Colour A: Depok 026 × 1 ball
- Colour B: Dubai 047 × 1 ball
- Colour C: Tokyo 061 × 1 ball

This is the only mitten pattern where you need to duplicate stitch part of the motif. Please see Basic Stitches: Duplicate Stitch and the tutorial video.

PATTERN

Using Colour A and 2.25mm (US 1) needles, cast on 60 (68) sts with the German Twisted Cast On (see Casting On and Off: German Twisted Cast On). Knit the first 2 rows flat:

Rows 1-2

*K2, p2; rep from * to end.
Continue knitting in the round.

Rounds 3-18

*K2, p2; rep from * to end.

Change to 2.5mm (US 1.5) needles.

Round 19

K all sts.

Round 20

Smaller size: K all sts. [60 sts]
Larger size: *kfb, k33; rep from * once more. [70 sts]

Join Colour B and later on Colour C and start knitting from Chart 1. Knit 1 repeat of Chart 1, then knit Rounds 1-2 once more for a total of 12 rounds.

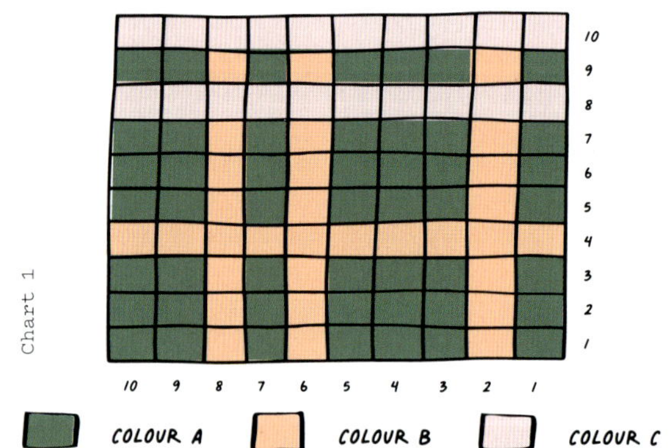

Read the chart from right to left and bottom to top. Each square counts as one stitch and the entire chart counts as one repeat of the pattern.

From the next round start increasing on one side for the thumb. Chart 2 contains a variation on the colourwork pattern. You'll see that some of the stitches are marked with X, these are stitches that you will duplicate stitch over at the end. Please note: Start knitting from Round 3 of Chart 2.

Rounds 4, 8 and 10 which normally are knitted in one single colour, are now worked using both Colours A and B. After knitting, use Colours B and C to duplicate stitch the marked stitches. I'll show you how to do this in the tutorial video.

Cut Colour C and continue knitting using just Colours A and B. Be sure to check Chart 3 as well as the written instructions. In Round 13 you'll be placing two stitch markers. The stitches in between those two markers are to be knitted according to the repeat in Chart 2.

Always pick up a Colour A strand for the m1 increase.

Increase round (Round 13)
K1A, pm, m1A. The m1-stitch now counts as the first stitch of the repeat shown in Chart 2.

Knit according to Chart 2 until 1 st left, then: m1A, pm, k1A. The last m1-stitch now counts as the last stitch in the repeat. [2 sts inc]

The stitch markers now mark the beginning and end of the colourwork section as shown in Chart 2. The stitches outside of the markers are your thumb sts as shown in Chart 3.

Straight round (even numbered rounds)
K all sts using A to marker, sm, work colourwork patt to marker, sm, k using A to end.

Increase round (odd numbered rounds)
K all sts using A to marker, m1A, sm, work colourwork patt to marker, sm, m1A, k using A to end.

Knit 1 round straight.

Repeat the increase round and straight round until you have increased 8 sts in total, 4 sts on either side of the colourwork section. Don't forget to knit the last straight round. [68 (78) sts]

COLOUR A COLOUR B

Chart 2

HAELEN HAT

HEERLEN HAT

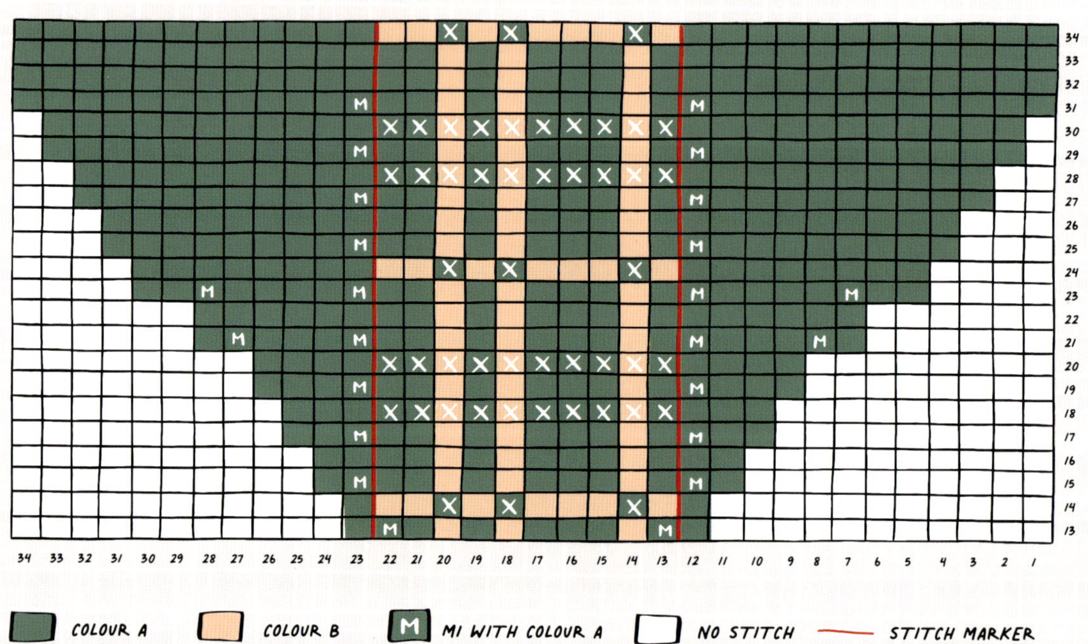

Chart 3 - thumb increases

The white squares in Chart 3 do not count as a stitch. Skip them and start the round at the first coloured square. Red lines mark the stitch marker placement.

In the following 2 increase rounds you increase 4 sts per round instead of 2 sts.

Increase round (Round 21)
K1A, m1A, k3A, m1A, sm, work colourwork patt to marker, sm, m1A, k3A, m1A, k1A.

Knit 1 round straight.

Increase round (Round 23)
K2A, m1A, k4A, m1A, sm, work colourwork patt to marker, sm, m1A, k4A, m1A, k2A.

Knit 1 round straight.

For the following increase rounds you increase 2 sts per round again.

Increase round
K all sts using A to marker, m1A, sm, work colourwork patt to marker, sm, m1A, k using A to end.

Knit 1 round straight.

Alternate between knitting an increase round and a straight round until you have increased 24 sts in total, 12 sts on either side of the colourwork section. [84 (94) sts]

After your last increase round knit 3 rounds straight in total. At this point you should have reached the end of Round 34 of Chart 3.

SPLIT FOR THE THUMB

Knit using A to marker, stranding Colour B at the back of your work.

Put thumb sts on waste yarn. The thumb sts are the first and last 12 sts of the round. Remove stitch markers.

Continue knitting according to Chart 1 over the remaining 60 (70) sts. Join in Colour C when you get to Round 8 of the chart.

Put a clip or clothes pin on the thumb to avoid laddering at the start of the round.

Continue knitting until you have knitted 5 repeats of the colourwork pattern, plus another repeat of Rounds 1-7, for a total of 57 rounds.

Change to 2.25mm (US 1) needles.

Cut Colours B and C and continue using only Colour A.

Right mitten

Next round: K all sts until 6 sts left. This will be the new start of the round. From this point, divide your sts evenly in two halves of 30 (35) sts across your needles.

Left mitten

Next round: K 6 sts. This will be the new start of the round. From this point, divide your sts evenly in two halves of 30 (35) sts across your needles.

Both mittens

Next round: K all sts.

Check that each half has the same number of sts. You decrease by 4 sts each decrease round.

Repeating pattern for decreases:

Round 1 (dec)

k1, ssk, k until last 3 sts of first half, k2tog, k1. Repeat for second half.

Rounds 2-4

K all sts.

Knit this repeat 3 times in total, you now have 48 (58) sts remaining.

Then:

Round 1 (dec)

k1, ssk, k until last 3 sts of first half, k2tog, k1. Repeat for second half.

Round 2

K all sts.

Knit this repeat 6 times in total, but omit the last straight round. You now have 24 (34) sts remaining.

There are 12 (17) sts on each needle. Seam closed with Kitchener stitch - see Casting on and Casting Off: Kitchener Stitch.

THUMB

See For All Mittens: Thumb.

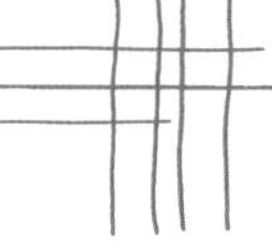

FINISHING

Using Colour B, duplicate stitch over the marked stitches of Round 4 of Chart 2, and use Colour C to duplicate stitch over the marked stitches of Rounds 8 and 10 (see Basic Stitches: Duplicate Stitch).

Use the cast-on tail of Colour A to seam the split in the cuff. For the thumb, use the Colour A tail at the base to sew the hole closed. Weave in all ends. Wash the mittens and lay flat to dry.

LEIDEN
·mittens·

MATERIALS

Scheepjes Metropolis
(200m/50g: 75% Extrafine Merino, 25% Nylon)

- Colour A: Liverpool 065 × 1 ball
- Colour B: Marseille 019 × 1 ball

Read the chart from right to left and bottom to top. Each square counts as one stitch and the entire chart counts as one repeat of the pattern.

The white squares in Chart 2 do not count as a stitch. Skip them and start the round at the first coloured square. Yellow lines mark the stitch marker placement.

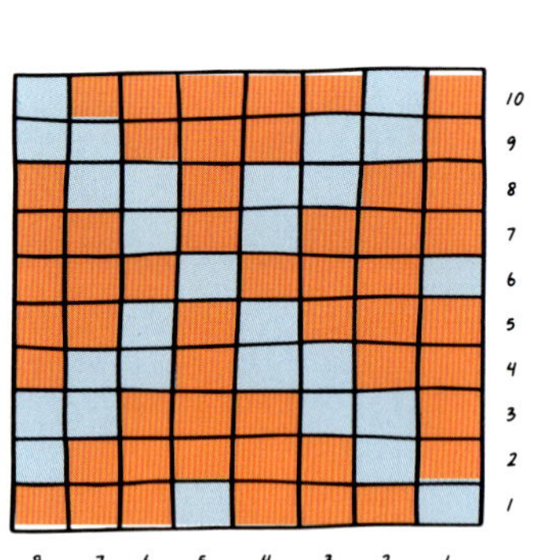

Chart 1

COLOUR A
COLOUR B
M1 WITH COLOUR A
NO STITCH
STITCH MARKER

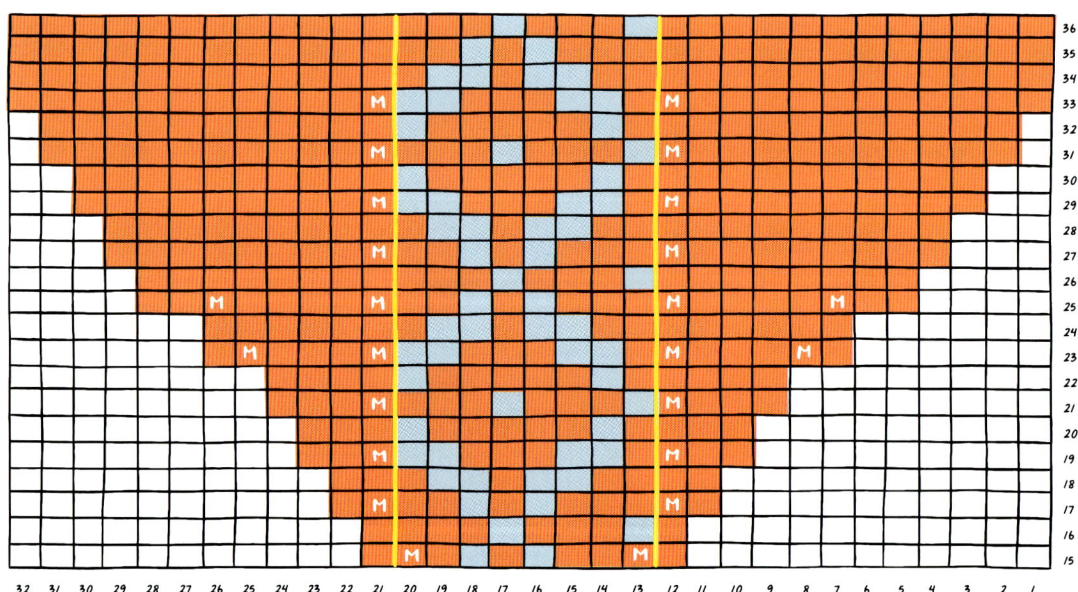

Chart 2 - thumb increases

PATTERN

Using Colour A and 2.25mm (US 1) needles, cast on 56 (64) sts with the German Twisted Cast On (see Casting On and Off: German Twisted Cast On).
Knit the first 2 rows flat:

Rows 1-2
*K2, p2; rep from * to end.

Rounds 3-18
*K2, p2; rep from * to end.

Change to 2.5mm (US 1.5) needles.

Rounds 19-20
K all sts.

Join Colour B and start knitting from Chart 1.

Knit 1 repeat of Chart 1, then knit Rounds 1-4 once more for a total of 14 rounds.

From the next round start increasing on one side for the thumb. Be sure to check Chart 2 as well as the instructions. In Round 15 you'll be placing two stitch markers. The stitches in between those two markers are knitted according to the repeat in Chart 1.

Tip

Always pick up a Colour A strand for the m1 increase.

Increase round (Round 15)
K1A, pm, m1A. The m1-stitch now counts as the first stitch of the repeat shown in Chart 1. Knit according to Chart 1 until 1 st left, then: m1A, pm, k1A. The last m1-stitch now counts as the last stitch in the repeat. [2 sts inc]

The stitch markers now mark the beginning and end of the colourwork section as shown in Chart 1. The stitches outside of the markers are your thumb sts as shown in Chart 2.

Straight round (even numbered rounds)
K all sts using A to marker, sm, work colourwork patt to marker, sm, k using A to end.

Increase round (odd numbered rounds)
K all sts using A to marker, m1A, sm, work colourwork patt to marker, sm, m1A, k using A to end.

Knit 1 round straight.

Repeat the increase round and straight round until you have increased 8 sts in total, 4 sts on either side of the colourwork section. Don't forget to knit the last straight round. [64 (72) sts]

In the following 2 increase rounds you increase 4 sts per round instead of 2 sts.

Increase round (Round 23)
K1A, m1A, k3A, m1A, sm, work colourwork patt to marker, sm, m1A, k3A, m1A, k1A.

Knit 1 round straight.

Increase round (Round 25)
K2A, m1A, k4A, m1A, sm, work colourwork patt to marker, sm, m1A, k4A, m1A, k2A.

Knit 1 round straight.

For the following increase rounds you increase 2 sts per round again.

Increase round
K all sts using A to marker, m1A, sm, work colourwork patt to marker, sm, m1A, k using A to end.

Knit 1 round straight.

Alternate between knitting an increase round and a straight round until you have increased 24 sts in total, 12 sts on either side of the colourwork section. [80 (88) sts]

After your last increase round knit 3 rounds straight in total. At this point you should have worked 3 whole repeats of the patt from Chart 1, plus 1 additional repeat of Rounds 1-6. In Chart 2 you have now reached the end of Round 36.

SPLIT FOR THE THUMB

Knit using A to marker, stranding Colour B at the back of your work. Put thumb sts on waste yarn. The thumb sts are the first and last 12 sts of the round. Remove stitch markers.

Continue knitting according to Chart 1 over the remaining 56 (64) sts.

Tip

Put a clip or clothes pin on the thumb to avoid laddering at the start of the round.

Continue knitting until you've knitted 5 repeats of Chart 1, plus 1 additional repeat of Rounds 1-6, which comes to 56 rounds.

Change to 2.25mm (US 1) needles.

Cut Colour B and continue using only Colour A.

Right mitten
Next round: K all sts until 6 sts left. This will be the new start of the round. From this point, divide your sts evenly in two halves of 28 (32) sts across your needles.

Left mitten
Next round: K 6 sts. This will be the new start of the round. From this point, divide your sts evenly in two halves of 28 (32) sts across your needles.

Both mittens
Next round: K all sts.
Check that each half has the same number of sts. You decrease by 4 sts each decrease round.

Repeating pattern for decreases:

Round 1 (dec)
K1, ssk, k until last 3 sts of first half, k2tog, k1. Repeat for second half.

Rounds 2-4
K all sts.

Knit this repeat 3 times in total, you now have 44 (52) sts remaining.

Then:

Round 1 (dec)
K1, ssk, k until last 3 sts of first half, k2tog, k1. Repeat for second half.

Round 2
K all sts.

Knit this repeat 5 times in total, but omit the last straight round. You now have 24 (32) sts remaining.

There are 12 (16) sts on each needle. Seam closed with Kitchener stitch - see Casting On and Casting Off: Kitchener Stitch.

THUMB AND FINISHING INSTRUCTIONS

See For All Mittens: Finishing.

HEERLEN
·mittens·

MATERIALS

Scheepjes Metropolis
(200m/50g: 75% Extrafine Merino, 25% Nylon)

- Colour A: Tokyo 061 × 1 ball
- Colour B: Dubai 047 × 1 ball
- Colour C: Philadelphia 007 × 1 ball

Read the chart from right to left and bottom to top. Each square counts as one stitch and the entire chart counts as one repeat of the pattern.

The white squares in Chart 2 do not count as a stitch. Skip them and start the round at the first coloured square. Red lines mark the stitch marker placement.

- COLOUR B
- COLOUR C
- M — M1 WITH COLOUR B
- NO STITCH
- STITCH MARKER

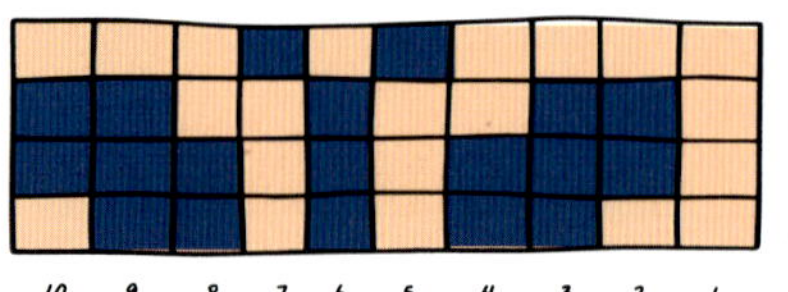

Chart 1

ALTERNATE COLOURWAY USING CANBERRA 031, MONTERREY 023 AND MANILA 012.

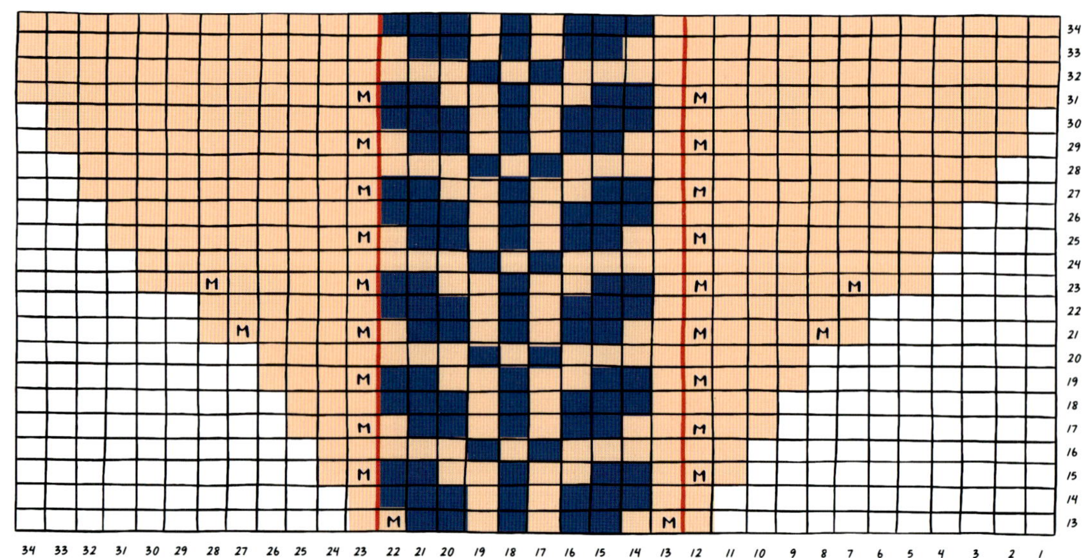

Chart 2 - thumb increases

PATTERN

Using Colour A and 2.25mm (US 1) needles, cast on 60 (68) sts with the German Twisted Cast On (see Casting On and Off: German Twisted Cast On). Knit the first 2 rows flat:

Rows 1-2
*K2, p2; rep from * to end.
Continue knitting in the round.

Rounds 3-18
*K2, p2; rep from * to end.

Change to 2.5mm (US 1.5) needles.

Round 19
K all sts.

Cut Colour A and join in Colour B.

Round 20
Smaller size: K all sts. [60 sts]
Larger size: *kfb, k33; rep from * once more. [70 sts]

Join Colour C and start knitting from Chart 1. Knit 3 repeats of Chart 1 for a total of 12 rounds.

From the next round start increasing on one side for the thumb. Be sure to check Chart 2 as well as the instructions. In Round 13 you'll be placing two stitch markers. The stitches in between those two markers are to be worked according to the repeat in Chart 1.

Tip

Always pick up a Colour B strand for the m1 increase.

Increase round (Round 13
K1B, pm, m1B. The m1-stitch now counts as the first stitch of the repeat shown in Chart 1. Knit according to Chart 1 until 1 st left, then: m1B, pm, k1B. The last m1-stitch now counts as the last stitch in the repeat. [2 sts inc]

The stitch markers now mark the beginning and end of the colourwork section as shown in Chart 1. The stitches outside of the markers are your thumb sts as shown in Chart 2.

Straight round (even numbered rounds)
K all sts using B to marker, sm, work colourwork patt to marker, sm, k using B to end.

Increase round (odd numbered rounds)
K all sts using B to marker, m1B, sm, work colourwork patt to marker, sm, m1B, k using B to end.

Knit 1 round straight.

Repeat the increase round and straight round until you have increased 8 sts in total, 4 sts on either side of the colourwork section. Don't forget to knit the last straight round. [68 (78) sts]

In the following 2 increase rounds you increase 4 sts per round instead of 2 sts.

Increase round (Round 21)
K1B, m1B, k3B, m1B, sm, work colourwork patt to marker, sm, m1B, k3B, m1B, k1B.

Knit 1 round straight.

Increase round (Round 23)
K2B, m1B, k4B, m1B, sm, work colourwork patt to marker, sm, m1B, k4B, m1B, k2B.

Knit 1 round straight.

For the following increase rounds you increase 2 sts per round again.

Increase round
K all sts using B to marker, m1B, sm, work colourwork patt to marker, sm, m1B, k using B to end.

Knit 1 round straight.

Alternate between knitting an increase round and a straight round until you have increased 24 sts in total, 12 sts on either side of the colourwork section. [84 (94) sts]

After your last increase round knit 3 rounds straight in total. At this point you should have worked 8 entire repeats of the patt from Chart 1, plus 1 additional repeat of Rounds 1-2. In Chart 2 you have now reached the end of Round 34.

SPLIT FOR THE THUMB

Knit using B to marker, stranding Colour C at the back of your work. Put thumb sts on waste yarn. The thumb sts are the first and last 12 sts of the round. Remove stitch markers.

Continue knitting according to Chart 1 over the remaining 60 (70) sts.

Tip

Put a clip or clothes pin on the thumb to avoid laddering at the start of the round.

Continue knitting until you've worked 13 repeats of Chart 1, plus 1 additional repeat of Rounds 1-3 for a total of 55 rounds.

Change to 2.25mm (US 1) needles.

Cut Colour C and continue using only Colour B.

Right mitten

Next round: K all sts until 6 sts left. This will be the new start of the round. From this point, divide your sts evenly in two halves of 30 (35) sts across your needles.

Left mitten

Next round: K 6 sts. This will be the new start of the round. From this point, divide your sts evenly in two halves of 30 (35) sts across your needles.

Both mittens

Next round: K all sts.

Check that each half has the same number of sts. You decrease by 4 sts each decrease round.

Repeating pattern for decreases:

Round 1 (dec)

k1, ssk, k until last 3 sts of first half, k2tog, k1. Repeat for second half.

Rounds 2-4

K all sts.

Knit this repeat 3 times in total, you now have 48 (58) sts remaining.

Then:

Round 1 (dec)

k1, ssk, k until last 3 sts of first half, k2tog, k1. Repeat for second half.

Round 2

K all sts.

Knit this repeat 6 times in total, but omit the last straight round. You now have 24 (34) sts remaining.

There are 12 (17) sts on each needle. Seam closed with Kitchener stitch - see Casting On and Casting Off: Kitchener Stitch.

THUMB AND FINISHING INSTRUCTIONS

See For All Mittens: Finishing.

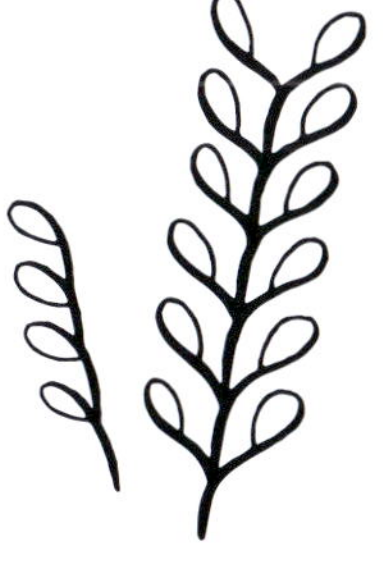

URMOND
·mittens·

MATERIALS

Scheepjes Metropolis
(200m/50g: 75% Extrafine Merino, 25% Nylon)

- Colour A: Bogotá 050 × 1 ball
- Colour B: Tokyo 061 × 1 ball

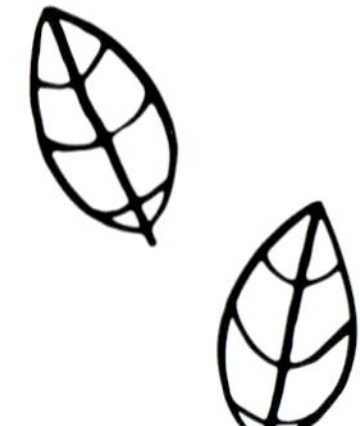

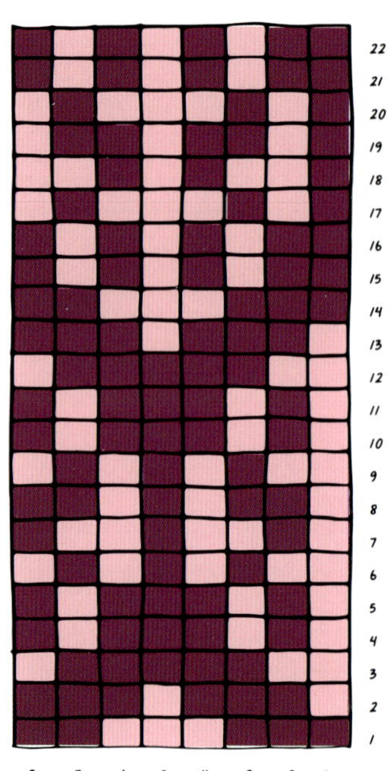

Chart 1

Read the chart from right to left and bottom to top. Each square counts as one stitch and the entire chart counts as one repeat of the pattern.

The white squares in Chart 2 do not count as a stitch. Skip them and start the round at the first coloured square. Yellow lines mark the stitch marker placement.

COLOUR A   COLOUR B   M1 WITH COLOUR A   NO STITCH   STITCH MARKER

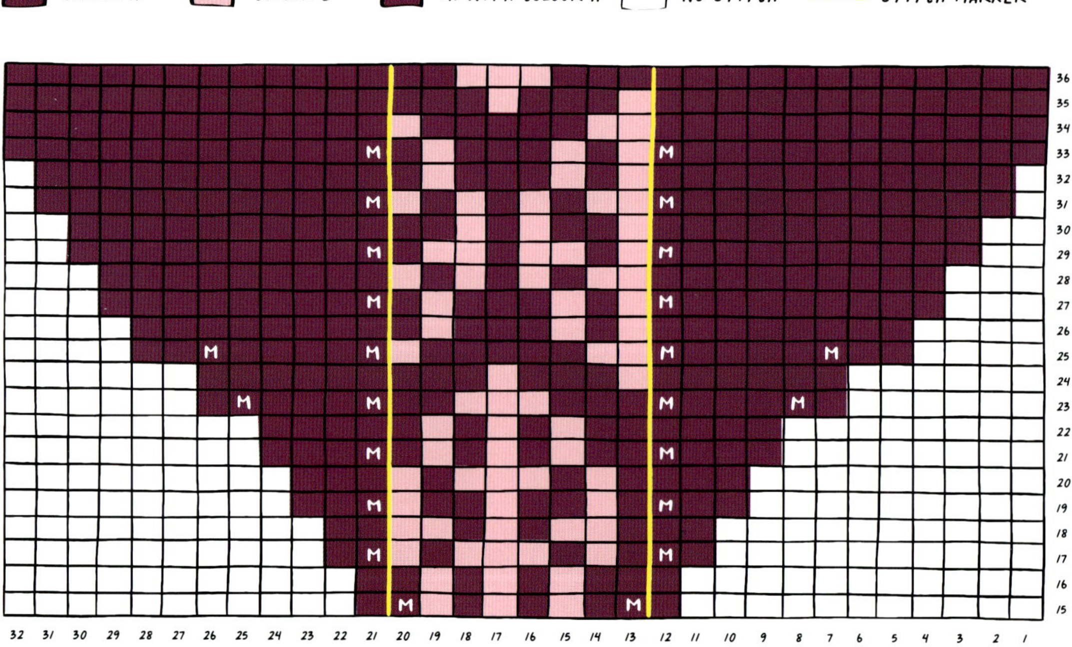

Chart 2 - thumb increases

PATTERN

Using Colour A and 2.25mm (US 1) needles, cast on 56 (64) sts using the German Twisted Cast On (see Casting On and Off: German Twisted Cast On).
Knit the first 2 rows flat:

Rows 1-2
*K2, p2; rep from * to end.
Continue knitting in the round.

Rounds 3-18
*K2, p2; rep from * to end.

Change to 2.5mm (US 1.5) needles.

Rounds 19-20
K all sts.

Join Colour B and start knitting from Chart 1. Knit Rounds 1-14 of Chart 1, for a total of 14 rounds.

From the next round start increasing on one side for the thumb. Be sure to check Chart 2 as well as the instructions. In Round 15 you'll be placing two stitch markers. The stitches in between those two markers are to be knitted according to the repeat in Chart 1.

Always pick up a Colour A strand for the m1 increase round (Round 15).

Increase round (Round 15)
K1A, pm, m1A. The m1-stitch now counts as the first stitch of the repeat shown in Chart 1. Knit according to Chart 1 until 1 st left, then: m1A, pm, k1A. The last m1-stitch now counts as the last stitch in the repeat. [2 sts inc]

The stitch markers now mark the beginning and end of the colourwork section as shown in Chart 1. The stitches outside of the markers are your thumb sts as shown in Chart 2.

Straight round (even numbered rounds)
K all sts using A to marker, sm, work colourwork patt to marker, sm, k using A to end.

Increase round (odd numbered rounds)
K all sts using A to marker, m1A, sm, work colourwork patt to marker, sm, m1A, k using A to end.

Knit 1 round straight.

Repeat the increase round and straight round until you have increased 8 sts in total, 4 sts on either side of the colourwork section. Don't forget to knit the last straight round. [64 (72) sts]

In the following 2 increase rounds you increase 4 sts per round instead of 2 sts.

Increase round (Round 23)
K1A, m1A, k3A, m1A, sm, work colourwork patt to marker, sm, m1A, k3A, m1A, k1A.

Knit 1 round straight.

Increase round (Round 25)
K2A, m1A, k4A, m1A, sm, work colourwork patt to marker, sm, m1A, k4A, m1A, k2A.

Knit 1 round straight.

For the following increase rounds you increase 2 sts per round again.

Increase round
K all sts using A to marker, m1A, sm, work colourwork patt to marker, sm, m1A, k using A to end.

Knit 1 round straight.

Alternate between knitting an increase round and a straight round until you have increased 24 sts in total, 12 sts on either side of the colourwork section. [80 (88) sts]

After your last increase round knit 3 rounds straight in total. At this point you should have worked 1 entire repeat of the patt from Chart 1, plus 1 additional repeat of Rounds 1-14. In Chart 2 you have now reached the end of Round 36.

SPLIT FOR THE THUMB

Knit using A to marker, stranding Colour B at the back of your work. Put thumb sts on waste yarn. The thumb sts are the first and last 12 sts of the round. Remove stitch markers.

Continue knitting according to Chart 1 over the remaining 56 (64) sts.

Put a clip or clothes pin on the thumb to avoid laddering at the start of the round.

Continue knitting until you've knitted 2 repeats of Chart 1, plus an additional repeat of Rounds 1-9, for a total of 53 rounds.

Change to 2.25mm (US 1) needles.

Cut Colour B and continue using only Colour A.

Right mitten

Next round: K all sts until 6 sts left. This will be the new start of the round. From this point, divide your sts evenly in two halves of 28 (32) sts across your needles.

Left mitten

Next round: K 6 sts. This will be the new start of the round. From this point, divide your sts evenly in two halves of 28 (32) sts across your needles.

Both mittens

Next round: K all sts.
Check that each half has the same number of sts. You decrease by 4 sts each decrease round.

Repeating pattern for decreases:
Round 1 (dec)
K1, ssk, k until last 3 sts of first half, k2tog, k1. Repeat for second half.

Rounds 2-4
K all sts.
Knit this repeat 3 times in total, you now have 44 (52) sts remaining.

Then:
Round 1 (dec)
K1, ssk, k until last 3 sts of first half, k2tog, k1. Repeat for second half.

Round 2
K all sts.

Knit this repeat 5 times in total, but omit the last straight round. You now have 24 (32) sts remaining.

There are 12 (16) sts on each needle. Seam closed with Kitchener stitch - see Casting On and Casting Off: Kitchener Stitch

THUMB & FINISHING INSTRUCTIONS

See For All Mittens: Finishing.

GENERAL INFORMATION

Sock knitting

These colourwork socks are knitted from the toe up using two colours. The motif is worked across the foot and the leg.

You knit a gusset on each side of the foot to allow for more room around the heel and ankle. The heel is a German Short Row Heel and is knitted back and forth using 'double stitches'. After knitting the leg you finish by knitting the cuff and binding off.

The pattern is written for circular needles, where the stitches are divided into two exact halves over the two needletips. In the pattern, Needle 1 refers to the first half of stitches and Needle 2 refers to the second half of the stitches.

When using double-pointed needles (DPNs), the stitches from Needle 1 and/or Needle 2 may be divided between multiple DPNs.

socks

I love to knit socks, and after years of knitting pair after pair this pattern is my favourite sock recipe so far. Toe up socks might sound daunting, but I actually find them easier to knit than cuff down socks. Please do watch the accompanying tutorial videos for extra guidance.

The sock patterns in this book incorporate a gusset - which looks like a triangle - on each side of the foot. Colourwork socks are less stretchy because of the yarn floats on the inside of your work. The gussets add a bit more room so that your socks are more comfortable to get on your feet.

If you have never knitted socks before, feel free to follow the pattern in just one colour at first. This way you can get used to the techniques involved without the added difficulty of the colourwork motif. Use the smaller size needles in this case.

FOR ALL SOCKS

Look for the motif you want to knit first, then return to this page for the general information and common parts of the pattern.

MATERIALS

Recommended needle size for circular or double-pointed needles

- 2.25mm (US 1) for the toe
- 2.5mm (US 1.5) for the rest

Recommended length circular needle

- 80cm (32in) for magic loop

Other materials

- Scissors
- Darning needle

TENSION

34 sts and 36 rounds of the stranded colourwork pattern on 2.5mm (US 1-2) needles measure 10×10cm (4×4in).

SIZES & MEASUREMENTS

This pattern contains instructions for six adult sizes.

	EU shoe sizes	US shoe sizes	UK shoe sizes	Length Toe & Foot*	Length Toe & Foot before Gusset start
1	35-36	5-6	2.5-3.5	18cm (7in)	11cm (4¼in)
2	37-38	6.5-7.5	4-5	19cm (7½in)	12cm (4¾in)
3	39-41	8-9.5	6-7	20cm (8in)	13cm (5in)
4	42-43	10-11	7.5-8	21cm (8¼in)	14cm (5½in)
5	44-45	12-12.5	9-10	22cm (8¾in)	15cm (6in)
6	46-47	13-14	10.5-12	23cm (9in)	16cm (6¼in)

Instructions for different sizes will be given in the pattern as 1(2;3) 4(5;6).

HEEL

The heel is worked only over the sts in between the gussets. Work using Colour A only.

Row 1 (WS)
Wyif, sl1p and lift the yarn upwards over the right-hand needle all the way to the back of your work, tugging firmly (forms a so-called 'double stitch'), wyif, p all sts to start of gusset, turn.

Row 2 (RS)
Wyif, sl1p and lift yarn to back as before, k all sts to next 'double stitch', turn.

Row 3
Wyif, sl1p and lift yarn to back as before, wyif, p all sts to next 'double stitch', turn.

Rep Rows 2 and 3 until you have 14(14;14)12(12;12) stitches left in between the double stitches, ending with a RS row.

Do not turn on your last RS row but knit first double st as if it were one st, turn.

Row 1 (WS)
Sl1p tugging firmly, p until next double stitch, p as if it were one st, turn.

Row 2 (RS)
Sl1p tugging firmly, k until next double stitch, k as if it were one st, turn.

Rep Rows 1 and 2 until all double sts have been worked. The last double st should be on a WS row, after that turn to RS.

CUFF

Cut Colour B. For the Heerlen socks also cut Colour A.

Using only Colour A (or Colour C for Heerlen socks):

Round 1
K all sts.

Round 2
P all sts.

Round 3
K all sts.

Rounds 4-10
*K1tbl, p1; rep from * to end. (7 rounds)

Bind off using Lori's Twisty Cast Off - see Casting On and Casting Off: Lori's Twisty Cast Off.

FINISHING

Wash and block your socks as explained in Abbreviations and Techniques: Washing and Blocking. Then weave in all ends.

WESSEM
socks

MATERIALS

Scheepjes Metropolis
(200m/50g: 75% Extrafine Merino, 25% Nylon)

- Colour A: Almaty 056 × 1 ball
- Colour B: Johannesburg 054 × 1 ball

PATTERN

TOE

Using Colour A and 2.25mm (US 1) needles, cast on 10(10;10) 12(12;12) sts each on Needles 1 and 2 using Judy's Magic Cast On - see Casting On and Casting Off: Judy's Magic Cast On. [20(20;20) 24(24;24) sts]

Toe round 1
K all sts.

Toe round 2 (inc)
*Kfb, k until 2 sts remain on Needle 1, kfb, k1, rep once from * for Needle 2. .

Knit Round 2 three more times. .

Then rep Rounds 1-2 until there are 64(64;64) 72(72;72) sts.

End with another Round 1.

FOOT

Change to 2.5mm (US 1.5) needles, join Colour B and start knitting in patt according to the Chart:

Continue knitting through Rounds 1-10 of the Chart until foot and toe together measure 11(12;13) 14(15;16)cm/4¼(4¾;5) 5½(6;6¼)in long. Then move on to Gusset.

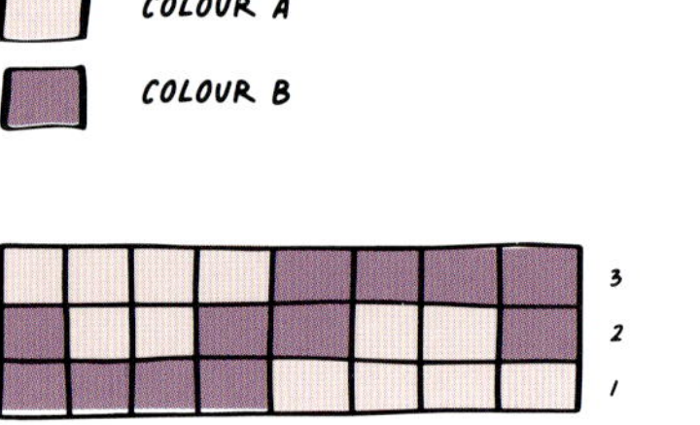

Chart

Read the chart from right to left and bottom to top. Each square counts as one stitch and the entire chart counts as one repeat of the pattern.

GUSSET

We create the gussets on Needle 2 by a series of m1-increases. Pick up a Colour B strand for the increase.

Gusset round 1 (inc)

K across Needle 1 in patt, turn to Needle 2. M1 using Colour B, k rest of Needle 2 in patt, m1 using Colour B. You have now increased 2 sts, 1 on either end of Needle 2.

Gusset round 2 and all even-numbered gusset rounds

K Needle 1 in patt, turn to Needle 2. Work gusset st(s) as they appear (k Colour A sts using A, Colour B sts using B), and k rest of Needle 2 in patt.

Gusset round 3 (inc)

K Needle 1 in patt, turn to Needle 2. M1 using Colour B, k rest of gusset st(s) as they appear, k rest Needle 2 in patt, m1 using Colour B.

For the rest of the gusset alternate between increase rounds and straight rounds.

After Gusset Round 3 you have 2 gusset sts on either side of Needle 2, all in Colour B. The next gusset sts are going to be inserted between those 2 Colour B sts. For each following gusset increase alternately between Colours A and B. For the third gusset st you'll use Colour A, for the next Colour B, and so on to create a striped gusset.

For the sts of the first gusset you knit the first st, then m1, then knit the remaining gusset sts. When you get to the sts of the second gusset you knit them until 1 left, m1, then knit the last st.

Continue alternating between straight rounds and increase rounds until you have 11(11;11) 13(13;13) sts for each gusset.

K in patt and work gusset sts as they appear until the sock measures 18(19;20) 21(22;23)cm/7(7½;8) 8¼(8¾;9)in long.

Next round

K Needle 1 in patt, turn to Needle 2, work the sts of the first gusset as they appear. Using only Colour A, k 32(32;32) 36(36;36) sts until you reach the second gusset. Cut Colour B, turn to work in rows.

HEEL

See instructions For All Socks: Heel.

HEEL FLAP

In this part we decrease the gusset sts and form the heel flap, a square panel at the back of the heel.

Row 1 (RS)
Sl1p, knit until 1 st before gap (gap will be obvious), ssk, turn work.

Row 2 (WS)
Sl1p, *p1, sl1p; rep from * to 1 st before gap, p2tog, turn work.

Row 3
Sl1p, *k1, sl1p; rep from * to 1 st before gap, ssk, turn work.

Rep Rows 2 and 3 until all gusset sts are decreased and you have 32(32;32) 36(36;36) sts on Needle 2.

The last decrease row is a WS row, turn to RS and:

Next row
K 32(32;32) 36(36;36) sts in Colour A.

Join Colour B and continue knitting from the Chart.

If necessary to avoid gaps on either side of the heel, pick up 1 st between Needle 1 and 2 and knit this st together with the next st. Do the same on the other side.

It is also possible to pick up an extra stitch and decrease it in the next round. If you do this, make sure you do not include the extra stitch in your chart.

LEG

Continue knitting until leg is 10cm (4in) long or of desired length. End with a Round 3 of the Chart.

Tip

If you want to knit longer socks, continue on a larger needle size.

Knit 1 more round using Colour B.

CUFF

See instructions For All Socks: Cuff.

FINISHING

See instructions For All Socks: Finishing.

ALTERNATE COLOURWAY USING MARRAKECH 051 AND KRAKÓW 064

HAELEN
socks

MATERIALS

Scheepjes Metropolis
(200m/50g: 75% Extrafine Merino, 25% Nylon)

- Colour A: Taipei 006 × 1 ball
- Colour B: Lagos 042 × 1 ball

PATTERN

TOE

Using Colour A and 2.25mm (US 1) needles, cast on 10(10;10) 12(12;12) sts each on Needle 1 and 2 using Judy's Magic Cast On - see Casting On and Casting Off: Judy's Magic Cast On. [20(20;20) 24(24;24) sts]

Toe round 1

K all sts.

Toe round 2 (inc)

*Kfb, k until 2 sts remain on Needle 1, kfb, k1, rep once from * for Needle 2.

Knit Round 2 three more times.

Then rep Rounds 1-2 until there are 70(70;70) 80(80;80) sts.

Please note: this means that for sizes 1, 2 and 3 you will have 36 sts on Needle 1, and 34 sts on Needle 2. It is helpful to mark the side with 36 sts with a stitch marker or waste yarn.

End with another Round 1.

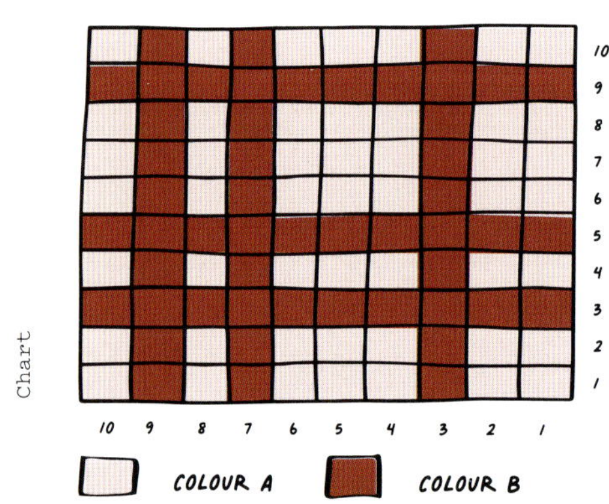

Read the chart from right to left and bottom to top. Each square counts as one stitch and the entire chart counts as one repeat of the pattern.

FOOT

Change to 2.5mm (US 1.5) needles, join Colour B and start knitting in patt according to the Chart.

Continue knitting through Rounds 1-10 of the Chart until foot and toe together measure 11(12;13) 14(15;16)cm/4¼(4¾;5) 5½(6;6¼)in long. Then move on to Gusset.

GUSSET

We create the gussets on Needle 2 by a series of m1-increases. Reminder for sizes 1-3: Needle 2 is the side with 34 sts. Pick up a Colour A strand for the increase.

Please note: Start your gusset on an even-numbered round of the Chart.

Gusset round 1 (inc)
K across Needle 1 in patt, turn to Needle 2. M1 using Colour A, k rest of Needle 2 in patt, m1 using Colour A. You have now increased 2 sts, 1 on either end of Needle 2.

Gusset round 2 and all even-numbered gusset rounds
K Needle 1 in patt, turn to Needle 2. Work gusset st(s) as they appear (k Colour A sts using A, Colour B sts using B), and k rest of Needle 2 in patt.

Please note: On Rounds 3, 5 and 9 of the Chart you're knitting a full round using Colour B. Any Colour A gusset sts should be slipped purlwise in these rounds.

Gusset round 3 (inc)
K Needle 1 in patt, turn to Needle 2. M1 using Colour A, k rest of gusset st(s) as they appear, k rest Needle 2 in patt, m1 using Colour A.

Continue to alternate between increase rounds and straight rounds.

After Gusset Round 3 you have 2 gusset sts on either side of Needle 2 in Colour A. The next gusset sts are going to be inserted between those 2 Colour A sts. For each next gusset increase alternately between Colours B and A. For the third gusset st use Colour B, for the next Colour A, and so on to create a striped gusset.

For the sts of the first gusset you knit the first st, then m1, then knit the remaining gusset sts. When you get to the sts of the second gusset you knit them until 1 left, m1, then knit the last st.

Continue alternating between straight rounds and increase rounds until you have 11(11;11) 13(13;13) sts for each gusset.

K in patt and work gusset sts as they appear until sock measures 18(19;20)21 (22;23)cm/7(7½;8) 8¼(8¾;9)in long.

Next round
Make sure you are on an even-numbered round of the Chart. K Needle 1 in patt, turn to Needle 2, work sts of first gusset as they appear. Using only Colour A, k 34(34;34) 40(40;40) sts until you reach the second gusset. Cut Colour B, turn to work in rows.

URMOND SOCKS

HEEL

See instructions For All Socks: Heel.

HEEL FLAP

In this part we decrease the gusset sts and form the heel flap, a square panel at the back of the heel.

Row 1 (RS)
Sl1p, knit until 1 st before gap (gap will be obvious), ssk, turn work.

Row 2 (WS)
Sl1p, *p1, sl1p; rep from * to 1 st before gap, p2tog, turn work.

Row 3
Sl1p, *k1, sl1p; rep from * to 1 st before gap, ssk, turn work.

Rep Rows 2 and 3 until all gusset sts are decreased and you have 34(34;34) 40(40;40) sts on Needle 2.

The last decrease row is a WS row, turn to RS and:

Next row
K 34(34;34) 40(40;40) sts in Colour A.

Join Colour B and continue knitting from the Chart.

If necessary to avoid gaps on either side of the heel, pick up 1 st between Needle 1 and 2 and knit this st together with the next st. Do the same on the other side.

It is also possible to pick up an extra stitch and decrease it in the next round. If you do this, make sure you do not include the extra stitch in your chart.

LEG

Continue knitting until leg is 10cm (4in) long or of desired length. End with a Round 4 or 10 of the Chart.

If you want to knit longer socks, continue on a larger needle size.

CUFF

See instructions For All Socks: Cuff.

FINISHING

See instructions For All Socks: Finishing.

LEIDEN
socks

MATERIALS

Scheepjes Metropolis
(200m/50g: 75% Extrafine Merino, 25% Nylon)

- Colour A: Milan 057 × 1 ball
- Colour B: Medan 005 × 1 ball

PATTERN

TOE

Using Colour A and 2.25mm (US 1) needles, cast on 10(10;10) 12(12;12) sts each on Needle 1 and 2 using Judy's Magic Cast On - see Casting On and Casting Off: Judy's Magic Cast On. [20(20;20) 24(24;24) sts]

Toe round 1
K all sts.

Toe round 2 (inc)
*Kfb, k until 2 sts remain on Needle 1, kfb, k1, rep once from * for Needle 2.

Knit Round 2 three more times.

Then rep Rounds 1-2 until there are 64(64;64) 72(72;72) sts.

End with another Round 1.

FOOT

Change to 2.5mm (US 1.5) needles, join Colour B and start knitting in patt according to the Chart.

Continue knitting through Rounds 1-3 of the Chart until foot and toe together measure 11(12;13) 14(15;16)cm/4¼(4¾;5) 5½(6;6¼)in long. Then move on to Gusset.

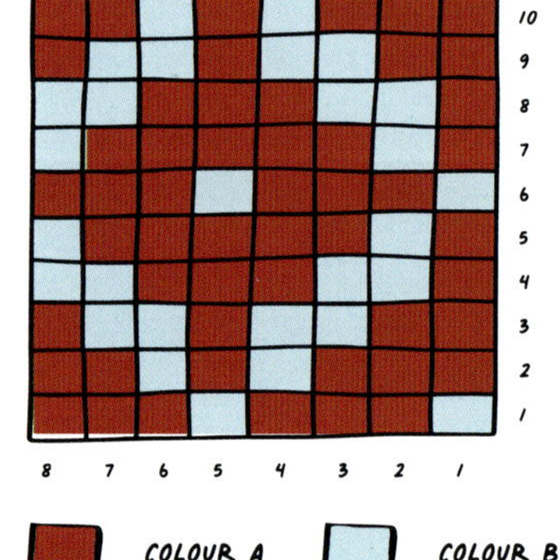

Read the chart from right to left and bottom to top. Each square counts as one stitch and the entire chart counts as one repeat of the pattern.

GUSSET

We create the gussets on Needle 2 by a series of m1-increases. Pick up a Colour A strand for the increase.

Gusset round 1 (inc)
K across Needle 1 in patt, turn to Needle 2. M1 using Colour A, k rest of Needle 2 in patt, m1 using Colour A. You have now increased 2 sts, 1 on either end of Needle 2.

Gusset round 2 and all even-numbered gusset rounds
K Needle 1 in patt, turn to Needle 2. Work gusset st(s) as they appear (k Colour A sts using A, Colour B sts using B), and k rest of Needle 2 in patt.

Gusset round 3 (inc)
K Needle 1 in patt, turn to Needle 2. M1 using Colour A, k rest of gusset st(s) as they appear, k rest Needle 2 in patt, m1 using Colour A.

For the rest of the gusset alternate between increase rounds and straight rounds.

After Gusset Round 3 you have 2 gusset sts on either side of Needle 2, all in Colour A. The next gusset sts are going to be inserted between those 2 Colour A sts. For each next gusset increase alternate between Colours B and A. For the third gusset st you'll use Colour B, for the next Colour A, and so on to create a striped gusset.

For the sts of the first gusset you knit the first st, then m1, then knit the remaining gusset sts. When you get to the sts of the second gusset you knit them until 1 left, m1, then knit the last st.

Continue alternating between straight rounds and increase rounds until you have 11(11;11) 13(13;13) sts for each gusset.

K in patt and work gusset sts as they appear until the sock measures 18(19;20) 21(22;23)cm/7(7½;8) 8¼(8¾;9)in long.

Next round
K Needle 1 in patt, turn to Needle 2, work the sts of the first gusset as they appear. Using only Colour A, k 32(32;32) 36(36;36) sts until you reach the second gusset. Cut Colour B, turn to work in rows.

HEEL

See instructions For All Socks: Heel.

HEEL FLAP

In this part we decrease the gusset sts and form the heelflap, a square panel at the back of the heel.

Row 1 (RS)
Sl1p, knit until 1 st before gap (gap will be obvious), ssk, turn work.

Row 2 (WS)
Sl1p, *p1, sl1p; rep from * to 1 st before gap, p2tog, turn work.

Row 3
Sl1p, *k1, sl1p; rep from * to 1 st before gap, ssk, turn work.

Rep Rows 2 and 3 until all gusset sts are decreased and you have 32(32;32) 36(36;36) sts on Needle 2.

The last decrease row is a WS row, turn to RS and:

Next row
K 32(32;32) 36(36;36) sts in Colour A.

Join Colour B and continue knitting from the Chart.

If necessary to avoid gaps on either side of the heel, pick up 1 st between Needle 1 and 2 and knit this st together with the next st. Do the same on the other side.

It is also possible to pick up an extra stitch and decrease it in the next round. If you do this, make sure you do not include the extra stitch in your chart.

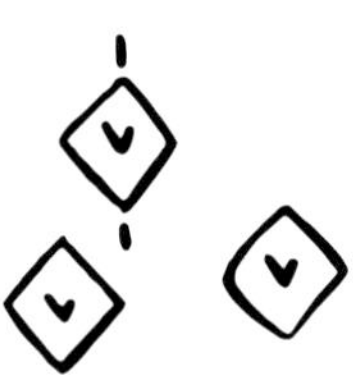

LEG

Continue knitting until leg is 10cm (4in) long or of desired length. End with a Round 1 or 6 of the Chart.

Tip

If you want to knit longer socks, continue on a larger needle size.

CUFF

See instructions For All Socks: Cuff.

FINISHING

See instructions For All Socks: Finishing.

HEERLEN
· socks ·

MATERIALS

Scheepjes Metropolis

(200m/50g: 75% Extrafine Merino, 25% Nylon)

- Colour A: Abu Dhabi 032 × 1 ball
- Colour B: Kabul 004 × 1 ball
- Colour C: Marseille 019 × 1 ball

PATTERN

TOE

Using Colour A and 2.25mm (US 1) needles, cast on 10(10;10) 12(12;12) sts each on Needle 1 and 2 using Judy's Magic Cast On - see Casting On and Casting Off: Judy's Magic Cast On. [20(20;20) 24(24;24) sts]

Toe round 1
K all sts.

Toe round 2 (inc)
*Kfb, k until 2 sts remain on Needle 1, kfb, k1, rep once from * for Needle 2.

Knit Round 2 three more times.

Then rep Rounds 1-2 until there are 70(70;70) 80(80;80) sts.

Please note: this means that for sizes 1, 2 and 3 you will have 36 sts on Needle 1, and 34 sts on Needle 2. It is helpful to mark the side with 36 sts with a stitch marker or waste yarn.

End with another Round 1.

FOOT

Change to 2.5mm (US 1.5) needles, join Colour B Cnd start knitting in patt according to the chart.

Continue knitting through Rounds 1-4 of the Chart until foot and toe together measure 11(12;13) 14(15;16)cm/4¼(4¾;5) 5½(6;6¼)in long. Then move on to Gusset.

Chart

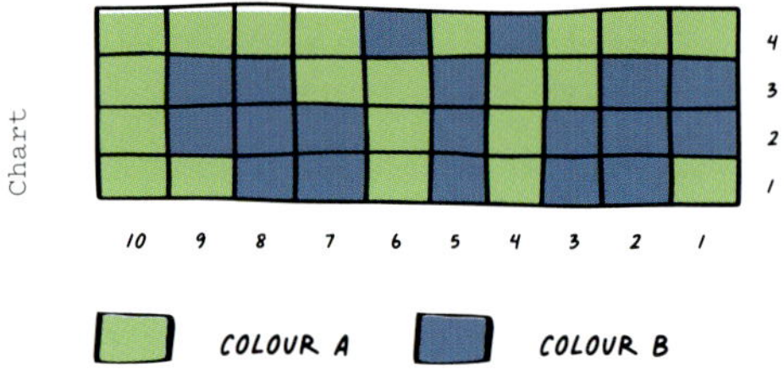

Read the chart from right to left and bottom to top. Each square counts as one stitch and the entire chart counts as one repeat of the pattern.

GUSSET

We create the gussets on Needle 2 by a series of m1-increases. Please note for sizes 1-3: Needle 2 is the side with 34 sts. Pick up a Colour A strand for the increase.

Gusset round 1 (inc)

K across Needle 1 in patt, turn to Needle 2. M1 using Colour A, k rest of Needle 2 in patt, m1 using Colour A. You have now increased 2 sts, 1 on either end of Needle 2.

Gusset round 2 and all even-numbered gusset rounds

K Needle 1 in patt, turn to Needle 2. Work gusset st(s) as they appear (k Colour A sts using A, Colour B sts using B), and k rest of Needle 2 in patt.

Gusset round 3 (inc)

K Needle 1 in patt, turn to Needle 2. M1 using Colour A, k rest of gusset st(s) as they appear, k rest Needle 2 in patt, m1 using Colour A.

For the rest of the gusset alternate between increase rounds and straight rounds.

After Gusset Round 3 you have 2 gusset sts on either side of Needle 2, all in Colour A. The next gusset sts are going to be inserted between those 2 Colour A sts. For each next gusset increase alternately between Colours B and A. For the third gusset st you'll use Colour B, for the next Colour A, and so on to create a striped gusset.

For the sts of the first gusset you knit the first st, then m1, then knit the remaining gusset sts. When you get to the sts of the second gusset you knit them until 1 left, m1, then knit the last st.

Continue alternating between straight rounds and increase rounds until you have 11(11;11) 13(13;13) sts for each gusset.

K in patt and work gusset sts as they appear until the sock measures 18(19;20) 21(22;23)cm/7(7½;8) 8¼(8¾;9)in long.

Next round

K Needle 1 in patt, turn to Needle 2, work the sts of the first gusset as they appear. Using only Colour A, k 34(34;34) 40(40;40) sts until you reach the second gusset. Cut Colour B, turn to work in rows.

HEEL

See instructions For All Socks: Heel.

HEEL FLAP

In this part we decrease the gusset sts and form the heel flap, a square panel at the back of the heel.

Row 1 (RS)
Sl1p, knit until 1 st before gap (gap will be obvious), ssk, turn work.

Row 2 (WS)
Sl1p, *p1, sl1p; rep from * to 1 st before gap, p2tog, turn work.

Row 3
Sl1p, *k1, sl1p; rep from * to 1 st before gap, ssk, turn work.

Rep Rows 2 and 3 until all gusset sts are decreased and you have 34(34;34) 40(40;40) sts on Needle 2.

The last decrease row is a WS row, turn to RS and:

Next row
K 34(34;34) 40(40;40) sts in Colour A.

Join Colour B and continue knitting from the Chart.

If necessary to avoid gaps on either side of the heel, pick up 1 st between Needle 1 and 2 and knit this st together with the next st. Do the same on the other side.

It is also possible to pick up an extra stitch and decrease it in the next round. If you do this, make sure you do not include the extra stitch in your chart.

LEG

Continue knitting until leg is 10cm (4in) long or of desired length. End with a Round 3 of the Chart.

If you want to knit longer socks, continue on a larger needle size.

Knit 1 more round using Colour A.

CUFF

See instructions For All Socks: Cuff.

FINISHING

See instructions For All Socks: Finishing.

URMOND
. socks .

MATERIALS

Scheepjes Metropolis
(200m/50g: 75% Extrafine Merino, 25% Nylon)

- Colour A: Buenos Aires 067 × 1 ball
- Colour B: Beirut 008 × 1 ball

PATTERN

TOE

Using Colour A and 2.25mm (US 1) needles, cast on 10(10;10) 12(12;12) sts each on Needle 1 and 2 using Judy's Magic Cast On – see Casting On and Casting Off: Judy's Magic Cast On. [20(20;20) 24(24;24) sts]

Toe round 1
K all sts.

Toe round 2 (inc)
*Kfb, k until 2 sts remain on Needle 1, kfb, k1, rep once from * for Needle 2.

Knit Round 2 three more times.

Then rep Rounds 1-2 until there are 64(64;64) 72(72;72) sts.

End with another Round 1.

Next round
Do not cut Colour A. Join Colour B and knit 1 round using Colour B.

FOOT

Change to 2.5mm (US 1.5) needles, start knitting in patt according to the Chart.

Continue knitting through Rounds 1-22 of the Chart until foot and toe together measure 11(12;13)14(15;16)cm/ 4¼(4¾;5)5½(6;6¼)in long. Then move on to Gusset.

COLOUR A

COLOUR B

Read the chart from right to left and bottom to top. Each square counts as one stitch and the entire chart counts as one repeat of the pattern.

GUSSET

We create the gussets on Needle 2 by a series of m1-increases. Pick up a Colour B strand for the increase.

Gusset round 1 (inc)

K across Needle 1 in patt, turn to Needle 2. M1 using Colour B, k rest of Needle 2 in patt, m1 using Colour B. You have now increased 2 sts, 1 on either end of Needle 2.

Gusset round 2 and all even-numbered gusset rounds

K Needle 1 in patt, turn to Needle 2. Work gusset st(s) as they appear (k Colour A sts using A, Colour B sts using B), and k rest of Needle 2 in patt.

Gusset round 3 (inc)

K Needle 1 in patt, turn to Needle 2. M1 using Colour B, k rest of gusset st(s) as they appear, k rest Needle 2 in patt, m1 using Colour B.

For the rest of the gusset alternate between increase rounds and straight rounds.

After Gusset Round 3 you have 2 gusset sts on either side of Needle 2, all in Colour B. The next gusset sts are going to be inserted between those 2 Colour B sts. For each next gusset increase alternately between Colours A and B. For the third gusset st you'll use Colour A, for the next Colour B, etc to create a striped gusset.

For the sts of the first gusset you knit the first st, then m1, then knit the remaining gusset sts. When you get to the sts of the second gusset you knit them until 1 left, m1, then knit the last st.

Continue alternating between straight rounds and increase rounds until you have 11(11;11) 13(13;13) sts for each gusset.

K in patt and work gusset sts as they appear until the sock measures 18(19;20) 21(22;23)cm/7(7½;8) 8¼(8¾;9.)in long.

Next round

K Needle 1 in patt, turn to Needle 2, work the sts of the first gusset as they appear. Using only Colour A, k 32(32;32) 36(36;36) sts until you reach the second gusset. Cut Colour B, turn to work in rows.

HEEL

See instructions For All Socks: Heel.

HEEL FLAP

In this part we decrease the gusset sts and form the heel flap, a square panel at the back of the heel.

Row 1 (RS)
Sl1p, k until 1 st before gap (gap will be obvious), ssk, turn work.

Row 2 (WS)
Sl1p, *p1, sl1p; rep from * to 1 st before gap, p2tog, turn work.

Row 3
Sl1p, *k1, sl1p; rep from * to 1 st before gap, ssk, turn work.

Rep Rows 2 and 3 until all gusset sts are decreased and you have 32(32;32) 36(36;36) sts on Needle 2.

The last decrease row is a WS row, turn to RS and:

Next row
K 32(32;32) 36(36;36) sts in Colour A.

Join Colour B and continue knitting from the Chart.

If necessary to avoid gaps on either side of the heel, pick up 1 st between Needle 1 and 2 and knit this st together with the next st. Do the same on the other side.

It is also possible to pick up an extra stitch and decrease it in the next round. If you do this, make sure you do not include the extra stitch in your chart.

LEG

Continue knitting until leg is 10cm (4in) long or of desired length. End with a Round 3 of the Chart.

Tip

If you want to knit longer socks, continue on a larger needle size.

Knit 1 more round using Colour B.

CUFF

See instructions For All Socks: Cuff.

FINISHING

See instructions For All Socks: Finishing.

Chapter 6

ABBREVIATIONS AND TECHNIQUES

ABBREVIATIONS

[...]	stitch count for this round/row
dec	decrease
inc	increase
k	knit
k1tbl	knit 1 st through back loop
k2tog	knit two together (decrease)
kfb	knit front and back loop of same st (increase)
p	purl
p2tog	purl 2 sts together (decrease)
patt	pattern
pm	place marker
rep	repeat
RS	right side
sl1p	slip 1 st purlwise
sm	slip marker
ssk	slip slip knit: slip next two sts knitwise one by one, insert left needle from left to right into these 2 sts and knit them together (decrease)
st(s)	stitch(es)
WS	wrong side
wyif	with yarn in front

SPECIAL ABBREVIATIONS

k1A	knit 1 stitch using Colour A
m1A	make 1 stitch using Colour A
k1B	knit 1 stitch using Colour B
m1B	make 1 stitch using Colour B

REPEAT PATTERNS

***...; rep from * to end** repeat the instructions after * to the end of the row/round.

(...) 2 times knit the instructions between brackets as many times as listed

How do you cast on stitches and what is the best cast off method? For many of my patterns I have a favourite cast on and cast off method. In this chapter you'll find my recommended methods for a stretchy cast on for hats, a seamless finish on mittens and more.

CASTING ON AND OFF

Slipknot

Hold yarn in left hand between thumb and middle finger. Loop yarn once around index finger to create a 'pretzel' (1). Put the right loop on your needle and pull tight (2).

Long tail cast on

The long tail cast on is the standard cast on method, which is used for the cowl patterns in this book. Start with a slipknot leaving a long tail. With the needle in your dominant hand, hold both yarn ends in your opposite hand with the tail going around your thumb and the ball-end around your index finger (1). Bring the needletip under the left thumb loop from left to right (2), and catch the left index finger loop from right to left (3). Bring this forward through the thumb loop (4), drop the loop from your thumb and pull the yarns tight (5). Repeat this for each stitch (6).

German twisted cast on

This cast on method creates a stretchy edge, perfect for hat brims and mitten cuffs. You will need a longer yarn tail compared to the long tail cast on. Start with a slipknot (1) and hold your yarn and needles as for the long tail cast on (2). Bring the needle under both strands on your thumb (3) and dip the needle down into the centre of the thumb loop (4). Catch the left index finger loop from right to left (5) and pull this through the small triangular gap of the thumb loop (6). Repeat this for each stitch (7).

SLIPKNOT

LONG TAIL CAST ON

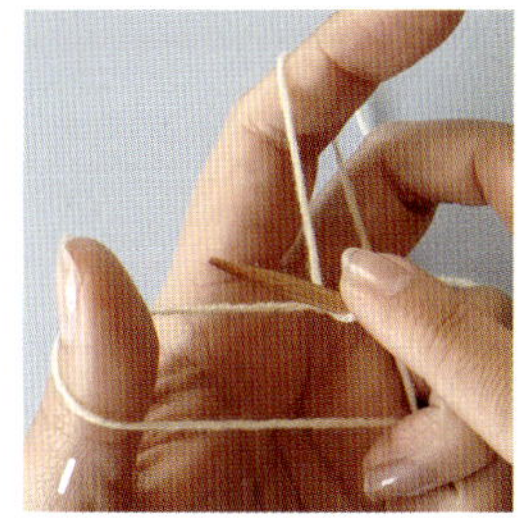

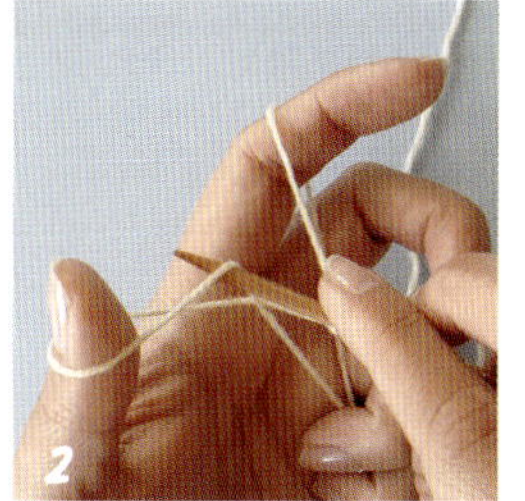

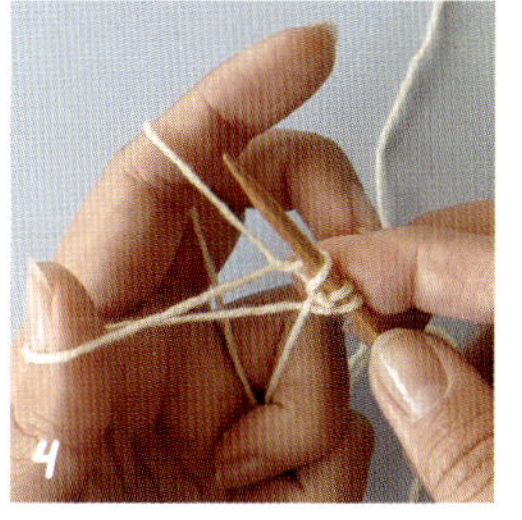

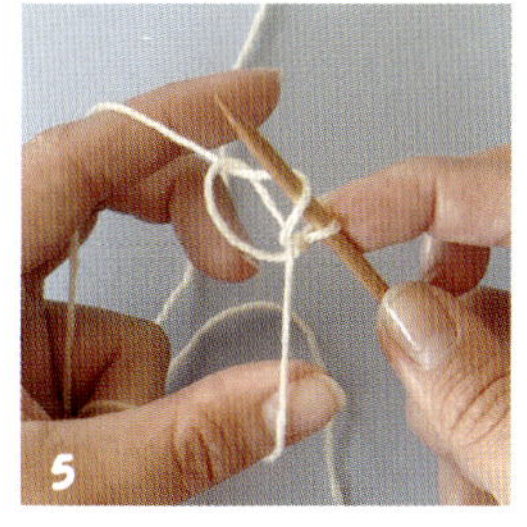

GERMAN TWISTED CAST ON

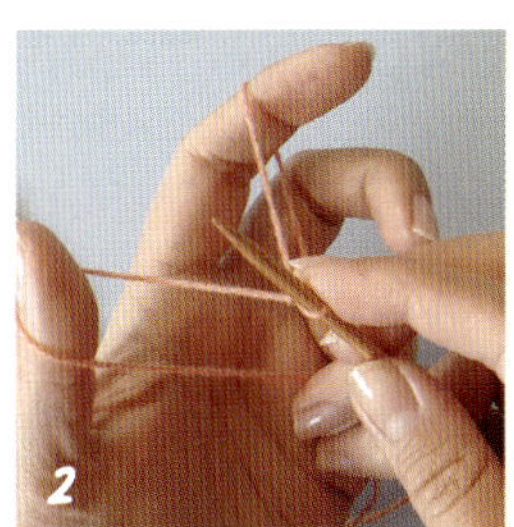

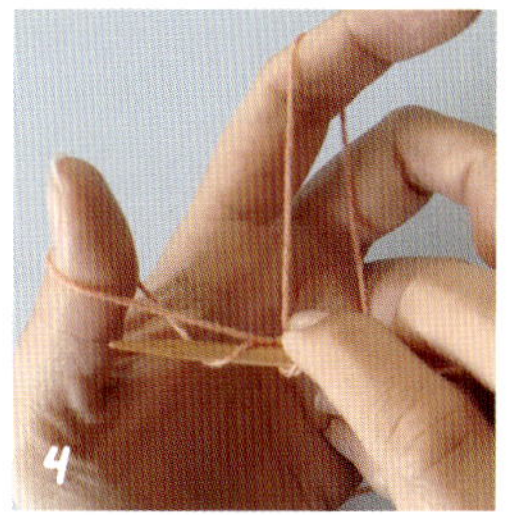

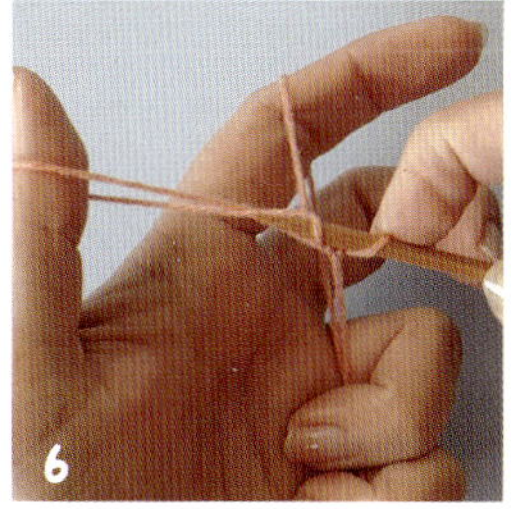

JUDY'S MAGIC CAST ON

Judy's magic cast on

This cast-on method was invented by Judy Becker and creates a beautiful seamless cast on for sock toes. Take both needletips in your dominant hand. Lay the yarn over the back needle with the yarn tail tucked between the needles and the ball-end going over the needle to the back (1). Twist the yarn ends anti-clockwise, holding the ball-end with your thumb and the yarn tail with your index finger (2). You now have 1 stitch on the back needle. With the index finger yarn, put a loop on the front needle (3). With the thumb yarn, put a loop on the back needle (4). Repeat these steps until you have the desired amount of stitches on each needle.

The last stitch you cast on will be quite loose, take care not to drop it off the needle (5). Rotate your work clockwise so that the needletips face the other way (6). Take the front needletip and pull it to the right so that the stitches are on the cable (7). Now you can bring both needletips together to knit the first half of the round (8). If your stitches appear twisted, knit them through the back loop instead.

When you have knitted all stitches of this first half (9), rotate your work clockwise again (10). Move the back needle back into your stitches and pull the front needle to the right (11). Now you can knit the second half of stitches (12).

Half mattress stitch

The half mattress stitch is used to seam live stitches to a cast on edge, and is used to finish the cowls in this book. Take your yarntail and put it through a darning needle (1). Insert needle as if to purl - from back to front - through the next stitch on your knitting needle and pull through (2). Find the corresponding stitch on your cast on edge and insert needle underneath both legs from right to left (3 and 4). Insert the needle from front to back through the stitch on your knitting needle (5) and let it slip off the knitting needle (6). Repeat this for every stitch (7 and 8).

HALF MATTRESS STITCH

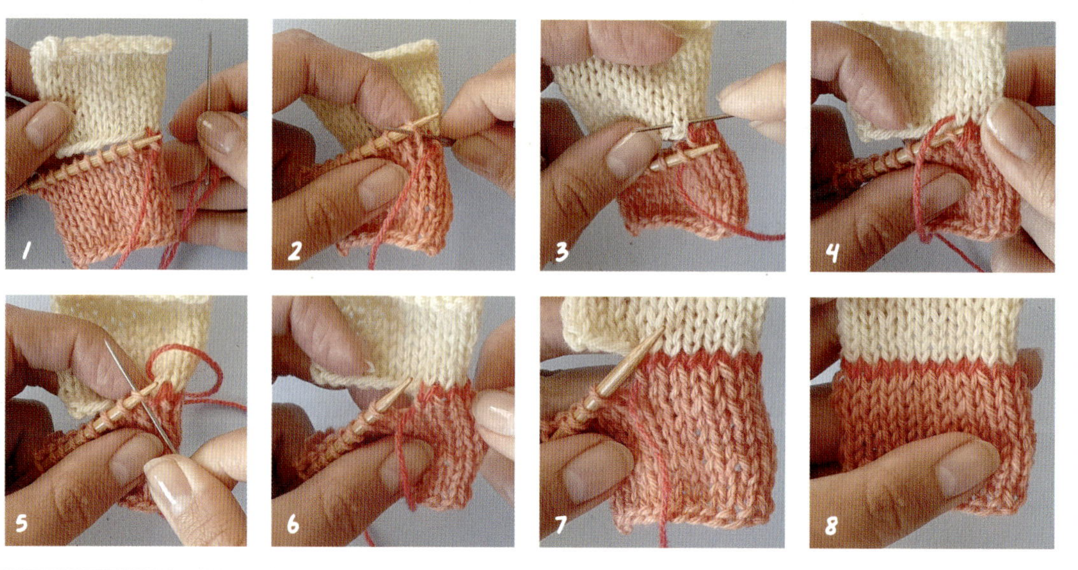

KITCHENER STITCH

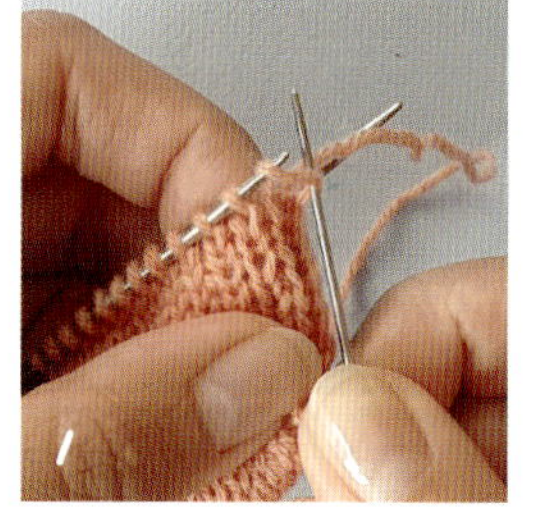

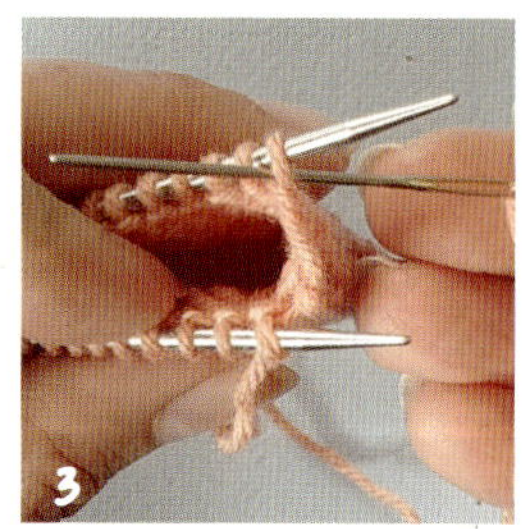

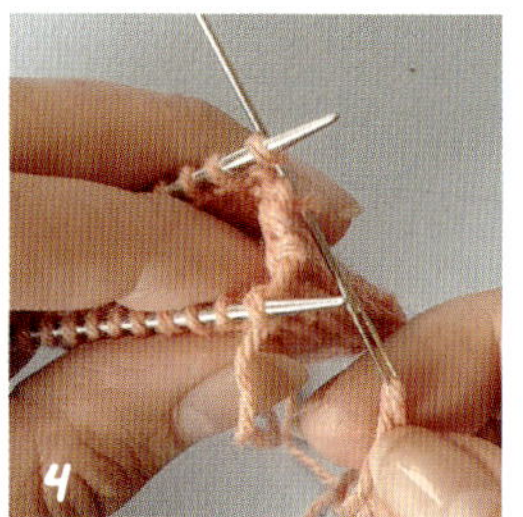

Kitchener stitch

The Kitchener stitch, also called grafting, is a method to seamlessly cast off stitches. The mitten pattern incorporates this technique to finish the top of the mitten. Take both needletips with each exactly half of the stitches. Cut the yarn at around 30cm (12in) and put it through a darning needle. With your darning needle, go through the first stitch on the front needle as if to knit and take it off the knitting needle (1). Then go through the second stitch on the front needle as if to purl and leave the stitch on the knitting needle (2).

Then go through the first stitch on the back needle as if to purl and take it off the knitting needle (3). Go through the second stitch on the back needle as if to knit, and leave it on the knitting needle (4). Repeat these steps until there are two stitches left on each needle. In the next repeat, also remove the second stitch off each needle. Then pull each stitch from right to left to neaten.

Lori's twisty cast off

Lorraine LeGrand created this stretchy cast off for ribbing. Knit the first stitch as normal. For each following stitch you rotate the working needle around its axis. I recommend using a separate knitting needle for this. It's important to hold your yarn away from the working needle to keep it from tangling. Please note the following is written for right-handed knitters; left-handed knitters will need to rotate the opposite direction. For each purl stitch you rotate the working needle anti-clockwise around its axis (1). Then purl the stitch and lift the first stitch over the second stitch (2). For each knit stitch you rotate the needle clockwise around its axis (3). Repeat this for every stitch (4).

LORI'S TWISTY CAST OFF

In this section you'll find instructions for knitting stitches and techniques using one colour. For instructions on colourwork knitting see Stranded Colourwork Knitting.

BASIC STITCHES

Knit stitch (k)

Hold the yarn at the back of your work (1). Insert the working needle into the next stitch from front to back, wrap the yarn around the working needle (2) and pull it forward through the stitch (3). Let the stitch slide off the holding needle (4).

Purl stitch (p)

Hold the yarn at the front of your work (1). Insert the working needle into the next stitch from back to front, wrap the yarn around the working needle (2) and pull it to the back through the stitch (3). Let the stitch slide off the holding needle (4).

If you're going from knit stitches to purl stitches or vice versa, don't forget to move the yarn to the back or to the front in between the needles.

Knitting two stitches together (k2tog)

Insert the working needle into the next two stitches from left to right (1). Wrap the yarn around the needle (2) and pull forward through the stitches (3). Let both stitches slide off the holding needle (4). You have now decreased one stitch.

Slip slip knit (ssk)

Slip the next two stitches knitwise one by one (1). Insert the holding needle back into the stitches from left to right (2), wrap the yarn around the working needle (3) and knit them together as if they were one stitch (4). You have now decreased one stitch.

KNIT STITCH

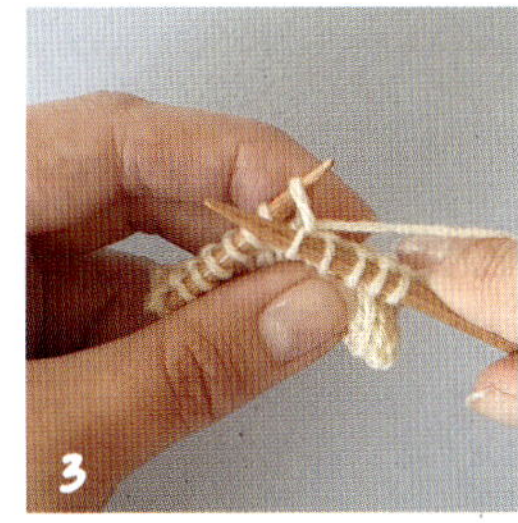

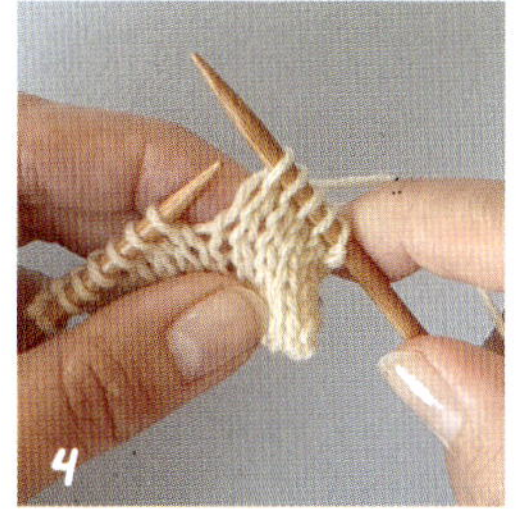

PURL STITCH

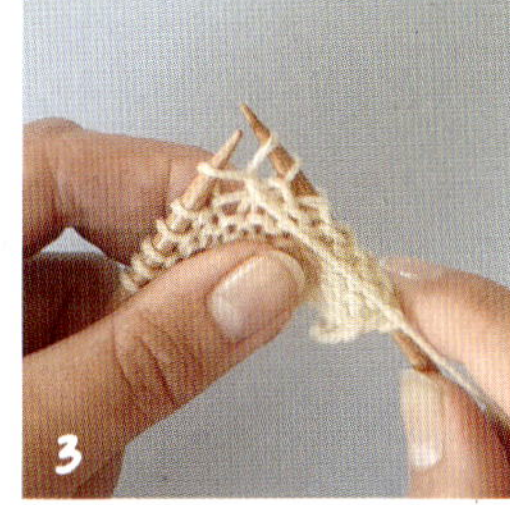

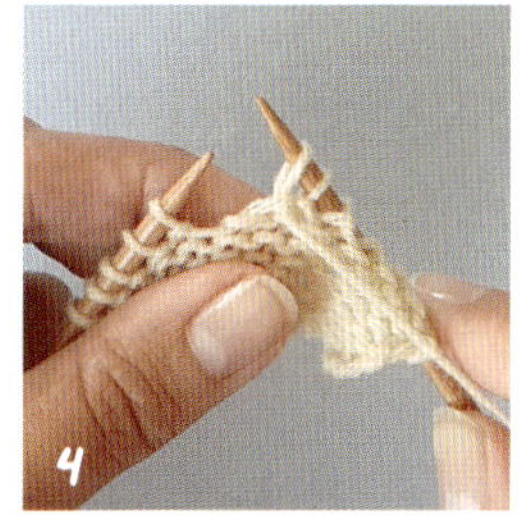

KNITTING TWO STITCHES TOGETHER

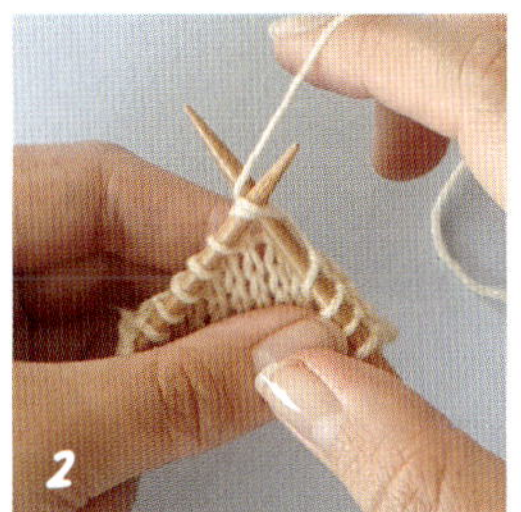

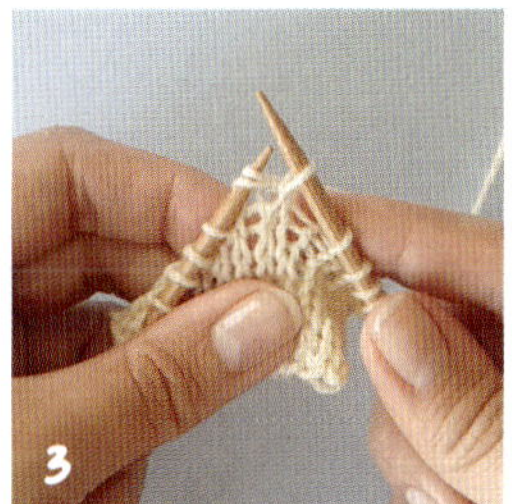

SLIP SLIP KNIT

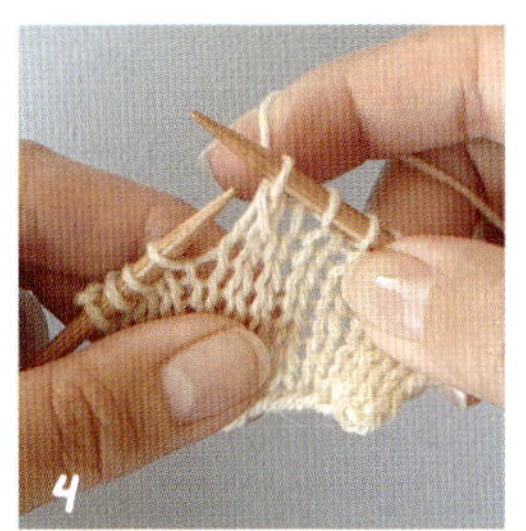

PURLING TWO STITCHES TOGETHER

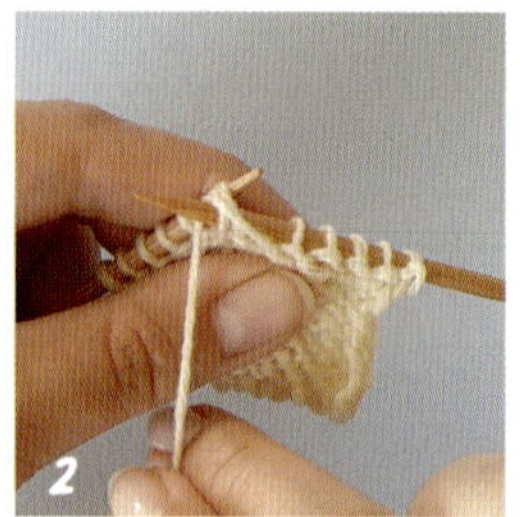

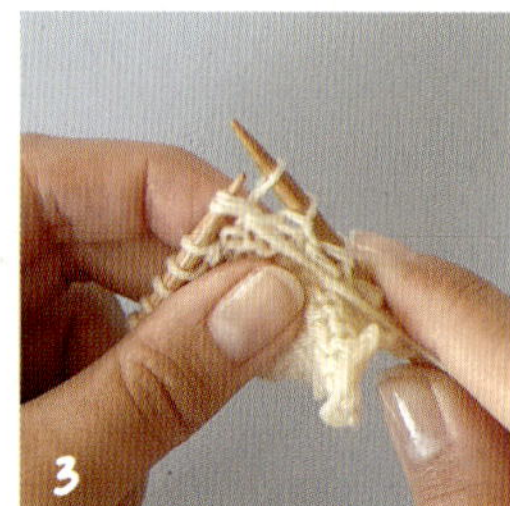

KNITTING INTO THE FRONT AND BACK OF THE SAME STITCH

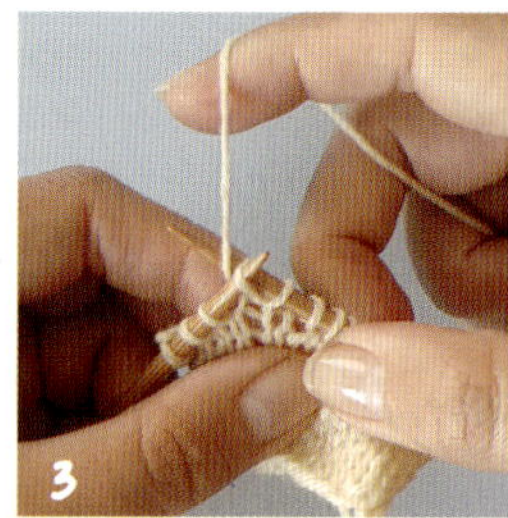

MAKE ONE STITCH

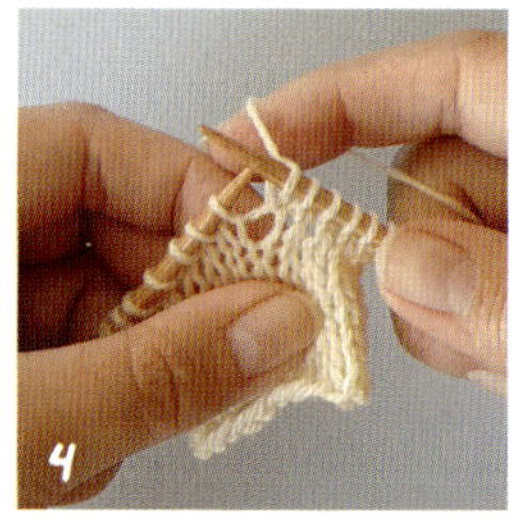

Purling two stitches together (p2tog)

Insert the working needle purlwise into the next two stitches (1). Wrap the yarn around the working needle (2) and pull to the back through the stitches (3). Let both stitches slide off the holding needle (4). You have now decreased one stitch.

Knitting into the front and back of the same stitch (kfb)

Knit one stitch, but don't let it slide off the holding needle yet (1). Insert the working needle into the back loop of the same stitch (2), wrap the yarn around the needle (3) and pull through the loop. Let the stitch slide off the holding needle (4). You have now increased one stitch.

Make one stitch (m1)

Spread your work so that you can see the horizontal bar in between the current stitch and the next (1). Put this loop on the left-hand needle with the right leg forward (2) and knit it through the back loop (3). Let the stitch slide off the holding needle (4). You have now increased one stitch.

Slipping a stitch knitwise (sl1k)

Insert the working needle from front to back into the next stitch, as if to knit, and slip it off the needle.

Slipping a stitch purlwise (sl1p)

Insert the working needle from back to front into the next stitch, as if to purl, and slip it off the needle.

SLIPPING A STITCH KNITWISE

SLIPPING A STITCH PURLWISE

DOUBLE STITCH

The double stitch is a technique used in the German Short Row Heel, and prevents holes from forming when turning your work. Depending on if you're on the purl side (wrong side) or the knit side (right side) of your work, here is how you make them:

Double stitch - Wrong Side:

Hold the yarn at the front of your work and insert the working needle from back to front through the next stitch (1). Slip the stitch onto the working needle (2). Lift the yarn up and over the working needle to the back of your work and pull tight until you see two loops on your needle (3). Bring the yarn forward in between both needles so you're in position to purl the next stitch (4).

Double stitch - Right Side:

Hold the yarn at the front of your work and insert the working needle from back to front through the next stitch (1). Slip the stitch onto the working needle (2). Lift the yarn up and over the working needle to the back of your work and pull tight until you see two loops on your needle (3). The loops will appear crossed on this side. Keep the yarn at the back of your work so you can knit the next stitch (4).

Magic Loop Knitting

Magic Loop is a technique where you can knit something with a small circumference on a long circular needle. I recommend knitting the first two rows of your project flat. Then move all stitches to the cable part of your circular needle (1). At the halfway point, pinch the cable and pull it out from between the stitches (2). It helps if you have exactly half the amount of stitches on each needle. Move the stitches to the needletips and make sure the working yarn is on the back needle (3). Also check to make sure your work is not twisted. Pull the back needletip out of the stitches so that those stitches are on the cable and move the needletips towards each other to knit (4).

DOUBLE STITCH – WRONG SIDE

1

2

3

4

DOUBLE STITCH – RIGHT SIDE

1

2

3

4

MAGIC LOOP

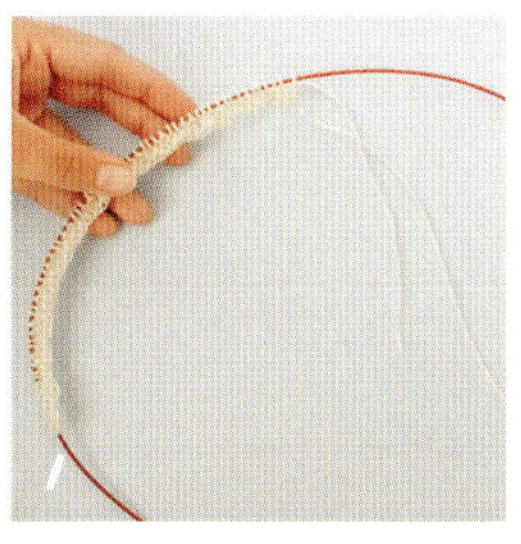
1

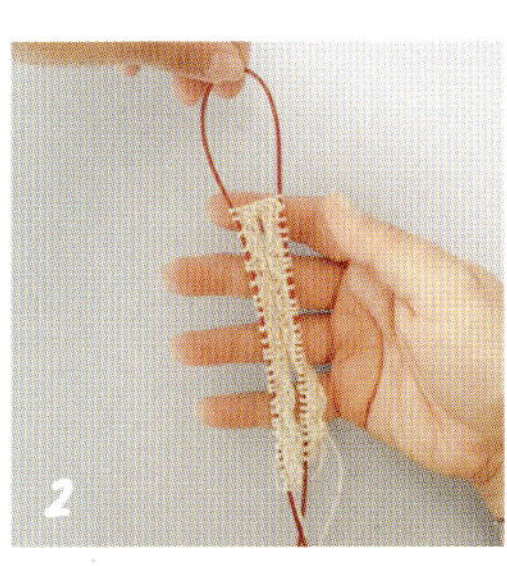
2

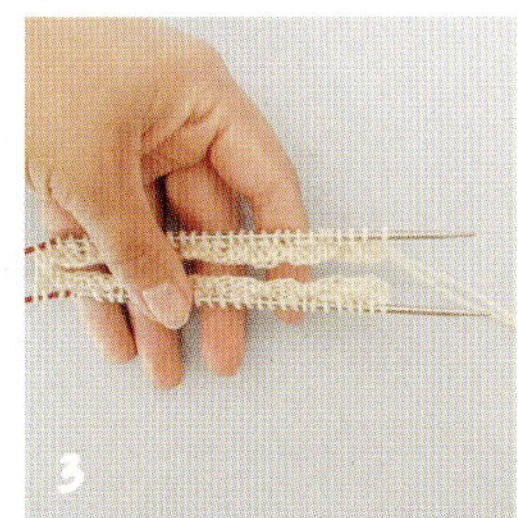
3

4

WEAVING IN YOUR ENDS

Take a sharp darning needle and thread your yarn through it. Turn to the back of your work and weave the needle diagonally through the purl bumps (1). I recommend piercing the stitches so that the yarn doesn't show on the right side. Do the same but in another direction (2). The yarn end is now secure and can be snipped off (3).

DUPLICATE STITCH

Duplicate stitching is when you are using a different colour yarn to embroider onto your knitting. This technique is used for the Haelen mittens.

Cut a length of yarn, take a blunt tapestry needle and thread the yarn (1). Locate the first stitch you want to embroider over and notice the 'V' shape. With your needle, come up through your knitting at the bottom of that V (2), and pull through. Insert the needle underneath both legs of the stitch directly above (3). Pull through and insert the needle back into the bottom of the stitch and pull through to the back (4). Repeat for every stitch you want to embroider over (5, 6, 7 and 8).

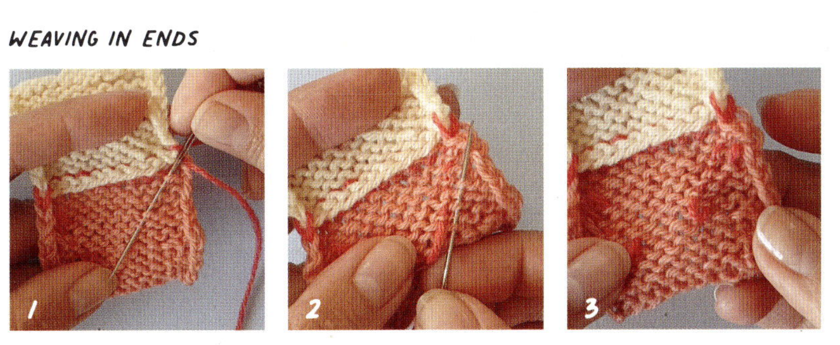
WEAVING IN ENDS
1
2
3

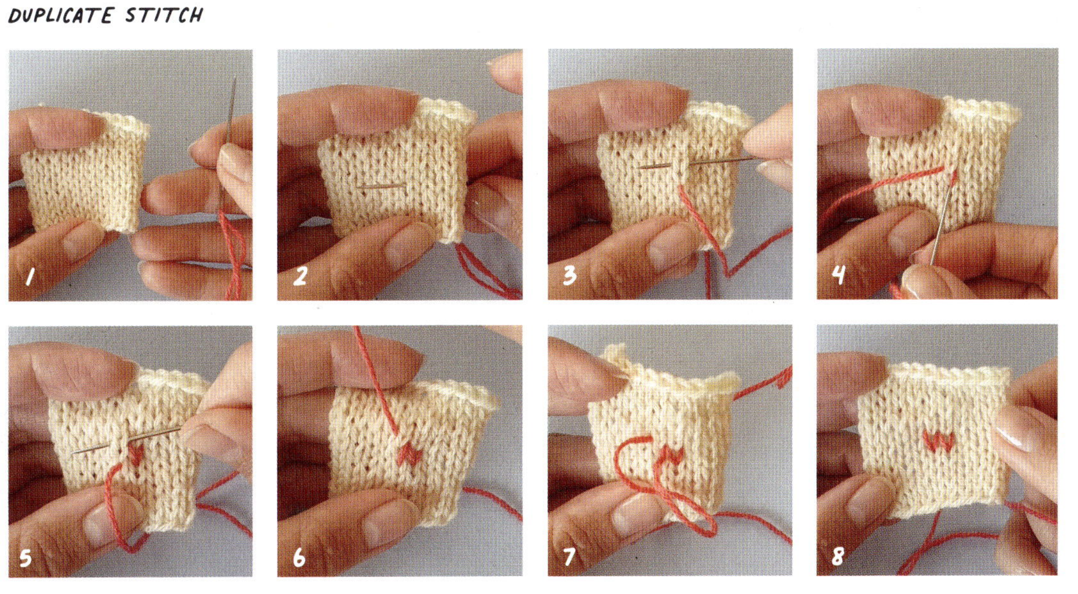
DUPLICATE STITCH
1
2
3
4
5
6
7
8

For stranded colourwork you use two or more colours to knit a repeating motif. Types of stranded knitting include regional styles such as Fair Isle motifs, Norwegian motifs, Estonian motifs and more. Stranded colourwork is the umbrella term for all underlying variations, and the term used throughout this book.

STRANDED COLOURWORK KNITTING

READING CHARTS

A big part of colourwork knitting is understanding charts. You'll see some examples on the opposite page. Read the chart from right to left and from bottom to top.

A chart is a visual representation of the knitting pattern, and each box or square stands for one stitch. The chart legend tells us what each box means. In Chart 1 on the opposite page Colour A stitches are represented by orange squares, and Colour B stitches by blue squares. Find the row count on the right, and the stitch count on the bottom of the chart. Usually the entire chart is one repeat of the pattern.

In some charts you'll also find symbols alongside the different colours. For Chart 2 the legend shows a symbol for 'K2togA', this means you are knitting two stitches together using Colour A.

Perhaps the most baffling symbol in charts is the 'no stitch' symbol, which is an empty square. Why is it there in the first place? You start Round 1 of this chart with 8 stitches in a repeat, but because of the decrease you end the round with 7 stitches in each repeat. In order to show this correctly in the chart there is a white square following the decrease. If you encounter 'no stitch' squares in a chart, skip them as if they aren't there at all, no matter if they're at the start of a row or in the middle.

If this is your first time reading charts, my advice is to take a piece of tape and stick it under or above the round you're working on. Blocking out the rest of the chart can help to focus on what you're doing right now. If the decrease or increase symbols and 'no stitch' squares are confusing, read the written instructions for that round and keep referring back to the chart. This way you'll get the hang of it in no time!

KNITTING WITH TWO COLOURS

All patterns in this book start with a single colour. You join in a second colour once you start knitting from the colourwork chart. Knit up until the first stitch you need to work with the second colour, and 'simply' knit it. This first stitch will be looser than the rest and can be tightened when weaving in the ends later.

You always have one background colour which forms the background to your motif, and the pattern colour which is used for the motif.

HOLDING ONE STRAND AT A TIME

ONE STRAND IN EACH HAND

BOTH STRANDS IN YOUR RIGHT HAND

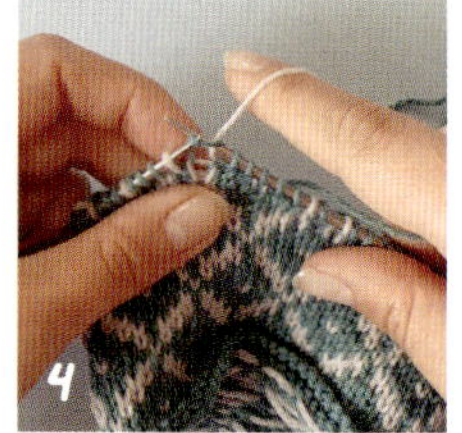

HOLDING YOUR YARNS

There are multiple ways to hold your yarns while knitting stranded colourwork. I'm showing you four different options, try them out and see what works best for you. Always hold the pattern colour to the left of the background colour, or vice versa for left-handed knitters.

Holding one strand at a time: this method is the most beginner-friendly. Pick up the colour you need for the next stitch or stitches (1), knit them, then drop the yarn to pick up the other colour (2 and 3). Do make sure the pattern colour stays on the left and the background colour on the right (4), otherwise your yarns will tangle.

One strand in each hand: this is the most common method of colourwork knitting, so definitely give it a try. Hold the pattern colour in your left hand. Do you crochet? Try holding the yarn as if you're crocheting. Take the background colour in your right hand (1). When you get to a background colour stitch, wrap the yarn around and knit it (2). When you get to a pattern colour stitch, use the working needle to make the stitch 'bigger' so you see the yarn behind it (3). Then scoop the yarn forward through the stitch (4) and let it slip off the needle.

Both strands in your right hand: hold both strands in your right hand with your index finger separating them. Again make sure the pattern colour is to the left of the background colour (1). Depending on the colour you need, use your index finger to wrap the background colour (2) or the pattern colour around the needle (3 and 4).

Both strands in your left hand: if you prefer continental style knitting, this method might be the one for you. Hold both strands in your left hand, with the knuckle of your index finger separating the two (1). Pattern colour on the left, background colour on the right. Insert the working needle into the next stitch (2), scoop up the colour you need (3) and pull it forward through the stitch (4).

BOTH STRANDS IN YOUR LEFT HAND

WRAPPING FLOATS

When you're knitting with two colours, the colour you're not using is stranded along the back of the work. The more stitches you knit in a single colour, the longer the other colour needs to be carried at the back. Sometimes it can be helpful to trap those strands - called 'floats' - so that they're not quite as long.

When to wrap your yarns

For beginner colourwork knitters I recommend wrapping the unused colour whenever you are knitting five stitches of one colour at a time. It's best to wrap your yarns halfway through, so on the third stitch in this case. As you get more experienced in stranded knitting you will feel less inclined to wrap your yarns, which is absolutely fine. It's best not to wrap your floats too often, such as every three stitches, because it will make your knitting quite stiff.

Another time you might want to catch your floats is when you're knitting magic loop, and you're going from one side of your work to the other. I recommend wrapping the unused yarn on the second stitch of the next side, or on the second to last stitch of the previous side.

Don't wrap your yarns at the same spot every round, this will be visible on the outside.

Wrapping the pattern colour

Insert the working needle into the next stitch and lay the pattern colour horizontally over the needle (1). Wrap the background colour around the needle (2). Pull the background colour through the stitch, ensuring to go underneath the wrapped pattern colour (3). Knit the next stitch as normal. The pattern colour is now wrapped (4).

Wrapping the background colour

Insert the working needle into the next stitch and wrap the background colour as if to knit (1). Then wrap the pattern colour as if to knit (2). Unwrap the background colour (3) and pull the pattern colour through the stitch (4).

Weaving in ends on colourwork knits is the same as weaving in ends for a solid coloured knitting project. Also see Basic Stitches: Weaving In Your Ends. Use a sharp darning needle to pierce through the stitches at the back of your work (1 and 2), or through the stranded floats. Do the same in another direction to secure the yarn (3 and 4).

SEE THE WRAPPED FLOAT HERE

WRAPPING THE PATTERN COLOUR

1

2

3

4

WRAPPING THE BACKGROUND COLOUR

1

2

3

4

WEAVING IN ENDS ON COLOURWORK KNITS

1

2

3

4

Blocking your work gives such a nice finish to your knitting, it truly is the cherry on top. Blocking usually means to wash your project, stretch it and leave it to dry. Stranded colourwork knits often look better after stretching, it defines the motifs and shows off your hard work.

WASHING AND BLOCKING

The first step to finishing your project is to wash it. Use tepid water and a bit of wool detergent, although this is optional. Leave it to sit for a while, then take it out of the water and squeeze most of the water out. Lay your knitting on a towel, roll it up and squeeze so that the towel absorbs the water.

Please take care to fully support the weight of your knit while it is wet. If you only hold part of it, the water weight can stretch and distort your project. When squeezing the water out do not wring it as this will also stretch the stitches. Colourwork projects often don't require precise pinning; patting the project flat and into shape works just fine.

For a cowl, it's best to block it before sewing it all up. At this stage it's still a flat piece of knitting, which dries quicker. If your needles aren't water resistant put the stitches on waste yarn before washing. Leave your cowl to dry flat on a drying rack, a yoga mat or kids' play mats.

Blocking a hat works a little differently. Leaving it to dry flat will cause fold lines and creases. So instead, drape it over a balloon or another round object. A balloon works especially well to stretch the colourwork motifs. Just take care to not make the balloon too big or it will overstretch the brim.

Mittens and socks can be washed and left to dry flat. My advice for blocking them is to reach in with your hand, and to spread out your fingers as you pull your hand out again. This way the mitten or sock will take its natural shape.

Acknowledgements

Writing my first book has been a true adventure from the very start, one that will bring me joy for years to come. I'm so proud of everyone who has been a part of this book, together we made something so beautiful!

Firstly I would like to thank Els for trusting me when she asked to work together on the original Dutch version of this book. I remember staring at my laptop utterly bewildered when I first read her proposal of publishing a book together. Me? Writing a book? Els saw something in me that I didn't see myself, and I thank her for her insights and patience.

Writing the translation for the English version of this book somehow feels even more surreal. A huge thank you to Sarah and the entire team at David & Charles, for helping to get this book out to knitters all around the world.

Kim, thank you for the stunning photography, I'm so glad to have had you on board for this journey. You fully captured my essence in the photos and your creative vision elevates the entire book. Sigrid, your eye for detail makes every page shine. From our very first chat we were very much in line with each other and I feel very grateful you took this project on. Marissa, I'm very thankful for your flexibility and for capturing the additional photos.

This book took almost two years to make and my family and friends have supported me immensely during that time. I'm very grateful to my parents, Tim, my family, family-in-law and Charlie. You gave me the confidence I needed when I didn't have it myself, and helped me overcome obstacles. You even modelled my knits during the photoshoot! Dad, Mum, Tim, Roel, Marie-lou, Jenny, Dirk, Eef, Charlie, you are all absolute superstars and seeing your faces in my book makes it all the more special to me.

Designing patterns is one thing, but making sure they are well written is quite another! Carna, Gea, Hilde, Kristina, Marie-Jozé, Marion, Yannic, many thanks for checking the patterns and knitting up the beautiful samples. I'm very grateful for your time, effort, and enthusiasm for the designs.

I would like to thank the Scheepjes team for sponsoring the yarns for this book. Even after so many years it's still a joy to work with your yarns and to create with so many colours.

And perhaps the most important, thank you to all members of the New Leaf Designs community. I'm grateful for your continuing support, understanding, passion and enthusiasm for craft.

A DAVID AND CHARLES BOOK

Original title: *Breien met Kleur*. Translated from the Dutch language.

www.unieboekspectrum.nl

David and Charles is an imprint of David and Charles, Ltd
Suite A, Tourism House, Pynes Hill, Exeter, EX2 5WS

EU GPSR Authorised Representative:
Logos Europe, 9 rue Nicolas Poussin, 17000, La Rochelle, France
Email: Contact@logoseurope.eu

First published in the UK and USA in 2026

A catalogue record for this book is available from the British Library.

ISBN-13: 9781446316542 paperback
ISBN-13: 9781446316559 EPUB

This book has been printed on paper from approved suppliers and made from pulp from sustainable sources.

Printed in China through Asia Pacific Offset for:
David and Charles, Ltd
Suite A, Tourism House, Pynes Hill, Exeter, EX2 5WS

10 9 8 7 6 5 4 3 2 1

David and Charles publishes high-quality books on a wide range of subjects. For more information visit www.davidandcharles.com.

Share your makes with us on social media using #dandcbooks and follow us on Facebook and Instagram by searching for @dandcbooks.

Layout of the digital edition of this book may vary depending on reader hardware and display settings.